Navigating Regulation D Private Offerings
What You Need to Know

D1474690

Jacqueline M. Benson

For additional copies or customer service inquiries, please e-mail west.customer.service@thomson.com.

ISBN 978-0-314-29388-6

Mat #41821590

ACKNOWLEDGMENT

I would like to thank David Roos, John Kellogg, Vicki and Wayne Benson, Matt Benson and Mike Morrow for taking the time to read through this book and give me their thoughts. Special thanks to my goldens, Connor and Midas, making sure my feet stayed warm while I worked. I would also like to thank the great folks at Moye White LLP for supporting my efforts to write this book.

DEDICATION

To my family, my husband, and my two furry boys, I could not have done this without your encouragement and support.

CONTENTS

Preface

This book is designed to help familiarize readers with the basic principles of private placement offerings pursuant to Regulation D of the Securities Act of 1933.[1] This is not a "how-to" guide and you should not participate in any private offering as an investor, issuer, or dealer without legal advice from experienced securities counsel. There are many nuances in the application of the securities laws that are not covered here and securities laws and regulatory guidance change frequently. Failure to comply with all of the requirements of state and federal law could result in rescission of the securities sale, state and federal private securities litigation, enforcement actions by state or federal regulatory agencies or even criminal enforcement actions. Further, sanctions in one offering can make you ineligible to engage in future offerings. Consider yourself duly warned.

To help illustrate certain points, the book uses the example of XYZ, Inc., a hypothetical corporation planning to sell 50,000 shares of common stock in a Regulation D offering. The securities laws apply to all forms of entity (corporations, partnerships, limited liability companies, etc.) and to all types of securities (common stock, preferred stock, partnership interests, limited liability company interests, certain debt instruments, etc.). Depending on the specifics of any given transaction, different documents or compliance steps may be necessary. Again, you should consult with your legal counsel to determine the best exemption, necessary documents and disclosure items and compliance plan for your specific transaction.

In this book, the term "issuer" refers to the company raising funds by selling securities.

---

[1] 17 C.F.R. §§ 230.501-230.506.

Introduction

Before we launch into the specifics of offerings under Regulation D, a little background on the securities law landscape may be helpful. First, "securities laws" typically refers to a broad body of laws that includes both federal and state statutes, regulations, interpretive guidance, and case law. Depending on the nature of any given transaction, federal laws as well as the laws of multiple states may apply. This overlapping combination of laws is one of the reasons that it can be challenging to understand securities laws.

The Securities Act of 1933[2] and the Securities Exchange Act of 1934[3] are the primary federal statutes governing offerings of securities. Both the Securities Act of 1933 and the Securities Exchange Act of 1934 have regulations that expand upon the statutory provisions. Regulation D is the primary federal regulation discussed in this book. The SEC also issues rule releases, no action letters, telephone interpretations and other interpretive guidance to provide further detail and explanation of the statutes and regulations. Most of this interpretive guidance is available to the public on the SEC website.

Another important concept is the distinction between "public" and "private" offerings. Both companies and offerings may be "public" or "private." A company is considered "public" if it has filed a registration statement with the Securities and Exchange Commission and that registration statement has gone effective. These companies are also called "publicly traded companies" because their stock is typically traded on an exchange or an over-the-counter market. Companies that have not gone through the process of becoming publicly traded are "privately held companies." Most of the companies in the United States are privately held.

---

[2] Securities Act of 1933, Pub. L. No. 73-22, 48 Stat. 74.
[3] Securities Exchange Act of 1934, Pub. L. No. 73-291, 48 Stat. 881.

Individual offerings can also be public or private. An offering that is registered with the Securities and Exchange Commission (and in certain circumstances, appropriate state regulatory agencies) is considered to be a public offering. Unregistered offerings may be private offerings if conducted in accordance with an applicable private offering exemption from registration. Unregistered offerings may also be exempt from registration pursuant to another exemption. Unregistered offerings that are not conducted in compliance with an exemption are illegal.

To further confuse the issue, publicly traded companies can conduct both public and private offerings. For example, if XYZ was a publicly traded company, it could raise money by conducting a registered offering. In the alternative, it could conduct a private offering to certain investors in compliance with Regulation D or another applicable exemption. Privately held companies can only conduct private offerings unless they are in the process of conducting an initial public offering to become publicly traded.

1

Section 5 and Registration Exemptions Generally

Section 5 of the Securities Act of 1933[4] provides that it is unlawful to directly or indirectly sell or deliver securities through interstate commerce unless a registration statement is in effect. This means every single sale of a security (even the sale of one share of stock for $0.17) must be registered with the Securities and Exchange Commission unless an exemption applies. There are two different types of exemptions to the Section 5 registration requirements. Section 3 of the Securities Act[5] contains exemptions for certain classes of securities, such as securities issued by the US government or certain non-profits or securities issued with bankruptcy court approval.

Section 4 of the Securities Act exempts certain types of transactions from Section 5 registration requirements. The most commonly used transactional exemptions are Sections 4(a)(1)[6] and 4(a)(2).

- Section 4(a)(1) exempts transactions conducted by a person[7] other than an issuer, underwriter, or dealer. This is typically used when a shareholder who is not an officer, director, or affiliate of an issuer sells their shares.

---

[4] Securities Act of 1933, Pub. L. No. 73-22, § 5, 48 Stat. 74.
[5] *Id.* § 3.
[6] *Id.* §§ 4(a)(1)-(2). These exemptions used to be known as Section 4(1) and 4(2) but all of Section 4 was renumbered in 2012 when the JOBs Act was enacted.
[7] In this context, the term "person" typically refers to both individuals and entities.

- Section 4(a)(2) exempts transactions by an issuer "not involving a public offering." Section 4(a)(2) is the basis for much of Regulation D and is discussed in detail in Chapter 2.
- Section 4(a)(3) exempts certain dealer transactions.[8]
- Section 4(a)(4) exempts unsolicited broker transactions executed upon customers' orders.[9]
- Section 4(a)(5) exempts sales of securities up to an aggregate of $5,000,000 solely to accredited investors provided there is no advertising or solicitation and the issuer files notice with the Commission.[10]
- Section 4(a)(6) exempts certain sales of up to $1,000,000 in any twelve-month period pursuant to the crowdfunding regulations. Crowdfunding is discussed briefly in Chapter 6.[11]

Another exemption that is sometimes referenced by practitioners is "Section 4(1)½." There is no Section 4(1)½ in the Securities Act, but the term is used for transactions that are a hybrid of Sections 4(a)(1) and 4(a)(2) for resales of securities by non-issuers through private offerings consistent with other private offering guidance.

For traditional issuers seeking to raise money through an unregistered securities offering, Section 4(a)(2) and the Regulation D exemptions promulgated under 4(a)(2) are the most commonly used exemptions to registration. The application and use of these exemptions is the focus of this book.

---

[8] Securities Act of 1933, Pub. L. No. 73-22, § 4(a)(3), 48 Stat. 74.
[9] *Id.* § 4(a)(4).
[10] *Id.* § 4(a)(5).
[11] *Id.* § 4(a)(6).

2

Section 4(a)(2) Private Placement Exemption

Section 4(a)(2) is the most frequently used transaction exemption from registration. It quite simply reads:

> The provisions of Section 5 shall not apply to—
> transactions by an issuer not involving any public offering.

This exemption is often referred to as the "private placement exemption" even though it does not actually use the words "private placement."

Conceptually, it makes sense that isolated private sales of securities should not require the same disclosure obligations as broad public offerings, however, the brevity of Section 4(a)(2) has created many interpretation issues. For instance, the text of Section 4(a)(2) does not define "public offering" or "private offering" or provide any guidance as to the distinction between the two. While most would generally agree that a private offer of securities to only one person is clearly a private offering and a widely advertised solicitation is a public offering, the areas between are far less clear.

Over time, the Securities and Exchange Commission and courts developed some basic parameters defining the characteristics of unregistered "private offerings." The most significant guidance was Release 33-4552[12] issued in 1962, which provides some criteria for the determination of whether an offering is public or private.

---

[12] Non-Public Offering Exemption, Securities Act Release No. 33-4552, 1962 WL 69540 (Nov. 6, 1962).

Current Section 4(a)(2) guidance generally focuses on the following factors when evaluating the nature of an offering:

- Number of offerees
- Nature of investors
- No advertising or solicitation
- Investment intent
- Disclosure of relevant information

Number of Offerees

The Commission has indicated that a private offering would include "an insubstantial number" of investors; however, neither the text of Section 4(a)(2), any definition in the Securities Act nor guidance from the Commission or the courts clearly defines the number of investors that would distinguish a private offering from a public one. In determining whether an offering involved a limited number of investors, the Commission considers both the number of purchasers and the number of offerees. For example, if XYZ offered its stock to 500 prospective investors, it likely would not be a private offering even if only two investors actually purchased the securities.

Nature of Investors

SEC guidance and judicial opinions have focused on two main concepts with respect to the nature of proposed investors. The first is whether the investors have the financial sophistication to evaluate the risks of the offering and make an investment decision. Sometimes, this is called the "sophistication" requirement. The Commission believes that unsophisticated investors need more regulatory protection and may be more susceptible to fraud. Note that the requirement to be sophisticated is distinct from the "accredited investor" concept that applies to certain offerings under Regulation D. Accredited investor status is based on the financial resources of the investor (net worth, income, etc.) and not their financial erudition.

The second consideration with respect to the nature of investors is their relationship with the issuer. In private offerings, the potential investors should have a pre-existing personal or business relationship with the principals of the issuer (or the broker selling the securities, if there is one). This pre-existing relationship should allow the issuer to better gauge whether the prospective investor has the financial resources and sophistication to invest in the offering. Further, if all investors are already within the professional or personal circle of the issuer's principals, there is no need to advertise the offering to strangers.

The bounds of this "pre-existing relationship" can be a bit nebulous and often extend beyond close friends and family to associates and friends of friends. In some cases, the manner in which the issuer met the proposed investor may be at issue. In our example, if the CEO of XYZ is playing golf with his friend Barry and Barry's neighbor Fred, and Barry mentions that Fred has a strong affinity for the widgets that XYZ sells and is looking for new investment opportunities, the CEO could discuss the offering with him (assuming the CEO reasonably believes Fred would be eligible to participate in the offering). On the other hand, if the CEO started cold calling members of the golf club that he did not know, that would likely be viewed as an improper solicitation.

No advertising or solicitation

SEC and judicial guidance has consistently stated that advertising and public solicitation of investors is inconsistent with private offerings. This makes intuitive sense. If you are advertising or conducting a public solicitation of investors, it looks more like a public offering than a private discussion between people with a pre-existing relationship. This concept ties to both the evaluation of the number of offerees and the requirement that investors in a private offering have a pre-existing relationship because if an issuer conducts advertising or broad solicitation, there will be a large number of offerees and there will not be a pre-existing relationship with the investors.

While the prohibition on advertising and solicitation applies to the Section 4(a)(2) exemption, there are certain types of exempted offerings under Regulation D that do not prohibit advertising or solicitation, as discussed further in Chapter 6.

Investment Intent and Transfer Restrictions

Another hallmark of a true private offering is that investors should intend to hold their investment for some period of time rather than immediately reselling the securities. This is important to prevent issuers from conducting veiled public offerings where securities are sold to a small number of investors in a private offering pursuant to Section 4(a)(2) and then immediately resold to the public in reliance on Section 4(a)(1).

To prevent these types of shenanigans, investors must demonstrate their investment intent by meeting certain holding periods before the shares can be resold. Holding periods are longer for affiliates of the issuer. This concept was incorporated into Rule 506[13] as part of the "restricted securities" rules requiring transfer restrictions on restricted securities. Transfer restrictions are typically documented as a legend on the stock certificate. Once the relevant holding periods are satisfied, investors can request to have the transfer restriction legend removed from their certificates pursuant to Rule 144. Investors will typically need to obtain a Rule 144 opinion from counsel confirming that all of the applicable provisions of Rule 144 are satisfied. Rule 144 of the Securities Act of 1933[14] provides a safe harbor for the sale of restricted securities provided certain holding periods, information disclosures, and other requirements are met.

Disclosure of Relevant Information

A critical component of both public and private offering regulations is the disclosure of key information about the issuer and the offering to prospective investors. For Section 4(a)(2) offerings, the issuer must provide the information necessary to evaluate the offering. This typically includes both a description of the terms of the offering itself and information about the issuer.

Through Regulation D, the Commission has expanded upon this concept by determining that unaccredited investors need more protection than their accredited brethren. Accordingly, if any of the offerees are unaccredited, the

---

[13] 17 C.F.R. § 230.506.
[14] 17 C.F.R. § 230.144.

issuer must provide specific and detailed disclosures as set forth in Regulation D. In contrast, the Commission has determined that sophisticated accredited investors know enough to protect themselves and to request the information that they need to make an investment decision. The specific disclosure requirements of Regulation D are described in Chapter 5.

In any event, issuers are obligated to provide fair, accurate, and complete information to their prospective investors. All information provided to investors under Section 4(a)(2),[15] Regulation D or otherwise, or that should be provided to investors, remains subject to both state and federal anti-fraud rules.

4(a)(2) Offerings

Issuers conducting private offerings in accordance with the concepts described above can rely on Section 4(a)(2) to exempt their offering from the registration requirements of Section 5.[16] No further filing or registration is necessary for federal purposes, although state compliance is still necessary (See Chapter 7).

For example, if XYZ decided to raise $100,000 by selling $50,000 worth of common stock to each of the CEO's Aunt Betty Lou and Elmer, his best friend since the third grade, and XYZ provided them with the necessary information about XYZ and the offering, and XYZ did not make any offer to any other proposed investor or engage in any advertising or solicitation, XYZ's offering would likely qualify as an exempt private offering pursuant to Section 4(a)(2). If XYZ also made offers to the CEO's neighbor Bob, his second cousin Wilma, the barista who runs the coffee cart in the lobby, all of the parents of the CEO's son's lacrosse team and everyone working out in the YMCA weight room on Tuesday afternoon, it is less clear whether the offering would still qualify for exemption under Section 4(a)(2).

The ambiguity surrounding Section 4(a)(2) made it very difficult for issuers to determine whether their offerings would be considered exempt

---

[15] Securities Act of 1933, Pub. L. No. 73-22, § 4(a)(2), 48 Stat. 74.
[16] *Id.* § 5.

by the Securities and Exchange Commission. This market uncertainty led the Commission to create Regulation D to provide more clearly defined parameters for a private offering exemption.

While Rule 504 and 505[17] were actually adopted under the authority granted to the SEC in Section 3(b) of the Securities Act[18] rather than Section 4(a)(2), most of the regulatory concepts of Section 4(a)(2) apply to all Regulation D exemptions.

[17] 17 C.F.R. §§ 230.504-230.505.
[18] Securities Act of 1933, Pub. L. No. 73-22, § 3(b), 48 Stat. 74.

3

The Regulation D Safe Harbor

In 1982, the Commission adopted Regulation D creating three exemptions from the registration requirements of the Securities Act. These new exemptions replaced certain existing exemptions as part of a more comprehensive set of private offering safe harbors. Rule 504 replaced Rule 240[19] and expanded it to permit sales of up to $500,000 of securities to an unlimited number of investors within a twelve-month period. Rule 505 replaced Rule 242[20] and expanded its limit to sales of $5,000,000 to up to thirty-five unaccredited investors and an unlimited number of accredited investors during a six-month period. Rule 506 replaced Rule 146[21] allowing an unlimited amount of sales to up to thirty-five unaccredited investors and unlimited number of accredited investors during any twelve-month period. Rule 501[22] contains definitions applicable to Regulation D, Rule 502[23] describes general conditions applicable to Regulation D offerings, and Rule 503[24] describes the Form D notice requirement.

Regulation D has undergone additional revisions over the years. Currently, Rule 504 permits offerings up to $1,000,000 every twelve months. Rule 505 permits offerings up to $5,000,000 to no more than thirty-five unaccredited investors every twelve months. Rule 506 permits offerings to no more than thirty-five unaccredited investors every twelve months without a dollar limit. Under Rule 505 and 506, there is no limit on the number of accredited investors that can participate.

---

[19] 17 C.F.R. § 230.240.
[20] *Id.* § 230.242.
[21] *Id.* § 230.146.
[22] *Id.* § 230.501.
[23] *Id.* § 230.502.
[24] *Id.* § 230.503.

The principal goal of Regulation D was to create clear parameters for the exemption of private offerings. Regulation D is often called a "safe harbor" because issuers automatically receive an exemption as long as they comply with all of the applicable requirements. Unlike registration statements that must be declared effective by the Securities and Exchange Commission, there is no requirement for the SEC to authorize, approve, or consent to Regulation D offerings.

Since its inception, Regulation D has become a critical mechanism for both small and large companies to raise capital. In 2012, more than $9 billion was raised in over 30,000 private offerings through Regulation D.[25] By comparison, there were 1,473 public debt transactions in 2012, the second most common mechanism for capital raising.[26] In 2013, over $1 trillion was raised in Regulation D Rule 506 offerings compared with $1.3 trillion raised in public offerings.[27]

There are a number of reasons why Regulation D is the most frequently utilized exemption for capital raises. First, since registration is not required, issuers do not need to go through the time-consuming and expensive process of obtaining audited financials, preparing and filing a registration statement with the SEC, undergoing the SEC review and approval process. The process of registering an offering often takes months and can cost hundreds of thousands of dollars. Further, Regulation D offerings can be conducted quickly. In theory, an issuer could commence a private offering in one day and close it the next; although it typically takes longer to decide on the structure for an offering, prepare the appropriate documentation, identify investors, and complete the closing.

Regulation D offerings are cost-efficient as well. Issuers may have costs associated with preparing disclosure materials for investors and engaging

---

[25] VLADIMIR IVANOV & SCOTT BAUGUESS, CAPITAL RAISING IN THE U.S.: AN ANALYSIS OF UNREGISTERED OFFERINGS USING THE REGULATION D EXEMPTION, 2009-2012 (2013), *available at* http://www.sec.gov/divisions/riskfin/whitepapers/dera-unregistered-offerings-reg-d.pdf.

[26] *Id.*

[27] Letter from Stephen M. Graham, Committee Co-Chair, Advisory Committee on Small and Emerging Companies, U.S. Securities & Exchange Commission to Mary Jo White, Chair, U.S. Securities & Exchange Commission on Recommendations Regarding the Accredited Investor Definition (Mar. 9, 2015), *available at* www.sec.gov/info/smallbus/acsec/acsec-accredited-investor-definition-recommendation-030415.pdf

counsel and other advisors to help with the offering, but there is no filing fee for filing Form D with the SEC. State filing fees for Regulation D offerings vary but are typically in the $50 to $500 range. Further, audited financial statements are not required for all Regulation D offerings, so companies do not need to undergo the time or expense of having their financials audited as they would for public offerings.

Another advantage is that Regulation D can be used by a wide range of companies. Approximately 60 percent of new offerings from 2009 to 2012 were conducted by operating companies, while the remaining 40 percent consisted of funds (hedge funds, private equity funds, venture capital funds, etc.), financial services, and real estate companies.[28] Further, both private and public companies take advantage of Regulation D offerings.

Finally, Regulation D offerings can be used to sell common or preferred stock, debt, partnership, or LLC interests or other securities. These factors make Regulation D the easiest and most efficient process for most companies to raise equity capital.

---

[28] *Id.*

4

Key Definitions and Conditions

This chapter provides some explanation of some of the key terms underpinning Regulation D. Understanding these terms is necessary to understand the exemptions.

Accredited Investor

One of the most important concepts incorporated into Regulation D is the "Accredited Investor." The Regulation D exemptions are premised on the idea that accredited investors need less protection than non-accredited investors because accredited investors are better able to evaluate and bear the risks of private placement investments. Accordingly, Regulation D favors offerings to accredited investors by requiring fewer disclosure obligations and no restrictions on the number of accredited investors in each offering. Further, for offerings pursuant to Rule 506(c),[29] advertising and public solicitation of investors is expressly permitted, so long as only accredited investors are allowed to participate in the offering (see discussion in Chapter 6).

This underlying premise makes sense in some situations, but less in others. For example, a wealthy executive with years of experience running a business may be in a better position to evaluate a securities offering and to absorb a loss of his or her investment than an entry-level clerk with few assets. On the other hand, a securities attorney with a business background, but lacking the assets or income to qualify as "accredited" may be far more capable of evaluating an offering than an uneducated, inexperienced twenty-year-old trust fund recipient with

---

[29] 17 C.F.R. § 230.506(c).

enough assets to qualify as "accredited." The sophisticated and prepared, but financially limited investor will be limited to private offerings allowing unaccredited investors or public offerings.

Rule 501(a)[30] describes both type of entities and individuals that qualify as "accredited." Rule 501(a)(1)-(3) and (7)-(8)[31] describes categories of accredited entities:

- Banks and savings and loan associations
- Registered brokers or dealers
- Insurance companies
- Registered investment companies
- Business development companies
- Small Business Investment Companies licensed by the SBA
- State or political subdivision or agency employee benefit plans with assets in excess of $5,000,000
- ERISA plans that: (i) are managed by a plan fiduciary which is a bank, savings and loan, insurance company or registered investment advisor; (ii) have more than $5,000,000 in assets; or (iii) if a self-directed plan, managed by exclusively accredited investors
- Private business development companies
- Organizations described by Section 501(c)(3)[32] of the Internal Revenue Code, corporations, Massachusetts or similar business trusts or partnership not formed for the specific purpose of acquiring the securities offered and holding more than $5,000,000 in assets
- Trusts with assets in excess of $5,000,000 not formed for the specific purpose of acquiring the offered securities whose purchase is directed by a sophisticated person
- Any entity in which all of the equity owners are accredited investors

Rule 501(a)(4)-(6)[33] describes categories of accredited individuals:

- Directors, executive officers, or general partners of the issuer or directors, executive officers, or general partners of the general partner of the issuer

---

[30] *Id.* § 230.501(a).
[31] *Id.* § 230.501(a)(1)-(3) and 230.501(a)(7)-(8).
[32] I.R.C. § 501(c)(3).
[33] 17 C.F.R. § 230.501(a)(4)-(6).

- Natural persons whose individual net worth, or joint net worth (excluding the value of the investor's primary residence) with such person's spouse, exceeds $1,000,000
- Individuals whose annual income exceeded $200,000 for the two most recent years and who expect to exceed that amount in the current year or individuals whose annual income combined with the income of their spouse exceeded $300,000 for the two most recent years and who expect to exceed that amount in the current year

While the basic definition of accredited investors has remained largely unchanged since it was originally proposed, there have been some recent notable changes. First, as a result of the real estate crisis and the Dodd-Frank[34] legislation, the definition of "net worth" in Rule 501(a)(5)[35] was revised in 2011 to expressly exclude both the value of the individual's primary residence and any debt securing such primary residence, so long as the estimated fair value of the home exceeds the amount of debt. As a result of this change, many investors whose primary asset was their residence were no longer able to qualify as accredited investors.

Second, the methodology for determining whether an investor qualifies as "accredited" was changed by the JOBs Act[36] for certain offerings. Historically, companies engaging in private placements relied on representations made by the investors in a subscription agreement confirming their accredited status, as well as the issuer's personal knowledge of the investor's financial situation. In connection with the JOBs Act provisions allowing solicitation and advertising in certain Rule 506 accredited-only offerings (discussed further in Chapter 6), the SEC has adopted rules requiring a higher level of diligence to confirm the accredited status of prospective investors for offerings under Rule 506(c).[37] The steps necessary to verify accredited status are described in more detail in Chapter 5.

---

[34] Dodd–Frank Act, Pub. L. No. 111–203, 124 Stat. 1376-2223 (2010).
[35] 17 C.F.R. § 230.501(a)(5).
[36] Jumpstart Our Business Startups Act, Pub. L. No. 112-106, 126 Stat. 306 (2012).
[37] 17 C.F.R. § 230.506(c).

Executive Officer

"Executive Officer" is defined in Rule 501(f).[38] Executive officers include the president, any vice president in charge of a principal business unit, division or function, or any other officer who performs a policy-making function for the issuer or issuer's subsidiary. Title alone does not determine who qualifies as an executive officer since responsibilities may vary widely from company to company. For example, a vice president might be an officer in charge with significant policy-making responsibility at one company or could be a manager-level position with no policy-making or managerial responsibility at another.

Distinguishing the executive officers of the issuer is important when determining whether an investor is accredited pursuant to Rule 501(a)(4).[39] Often, small start-up companies may have a small handful of founders, who also serve as officers of the company (and often board members) and qualify as "Executive Officer" as they maintain all of the policy-making and management responsibility for the company.

Sophisticated Investors and Purchaser Representatives

Rule 506 requires that all non-accredited investors be sophisticated investors, either alone or in connection with their purchaser representative. The term "sophisticated" is not actually used in Rule 506, but the rule generally refers to the provisions in Rule 506(b)(2)(ii)[40] that require the investor to have "such knowledge and experience in financial and business matters that he is capable of evaluating the merits and risks of the prospective investment, or the issuer reasonably believes immediately prior to making any sale that such purchaser comes within this description."

If an investor is not personally "sophisticated," he could still purchase securities in a Rule 506 private placement if he has a sophisticated Purchaser Representative. This occurs most commonly when a parent or grandparent purchases securities on behalf of minor children or handles investment

---

[38] *Id.* § 230.501(f).
[39] *Id.* § 230.501(a)(4).
[40] *Id.* § 230.506(b)(2)(ii).

responsibilities for other family members. Purchaser Representatives should be acknowledged by the investor in writing and should disclose any relationship between himself and his affiliates and the issuer and the issuer's affiliates within the previous two years, including any compensation received as a result of such relationship.

Purchaser Representatives cannot be affiliates, officers, directors, employees, or beneficial owners of the issuer, unless the purchaser is:

(i)   a relative by blood, marriage, or adoption;

(ii)   a trust or estate in which the purchaser representative is the trustee, executor, or has similar responsibility or in which the purchaser representative and its affiliates own more than 50 percent of the beneficial interest; or

(iii)   an organization in which the purchaser representative and its affiliates own more than 50 percent of the equity securities.

This restriction is designed to prevent principals of the issuer from claiming purchaser representative status with respect to purchases of securities by unrelated investors that would not otherwise be qualified to make an investment decision.

5

Key Conditions for Regulation D Offerings

Chapter 5 contains a discussion of some conditions and concepts applicable to Regulation D offerings. Understanding these concepts is key to interpreting the exemptions discussed in Chapter 6.

Bad Boy Provisions

Regulation A[41] is another exemption from the Section 5 registration requirements. It includes certain disqualifying provisions, often called "Bad Boy Provisions," preventing an issuer from relying on the Regulation A exemption if the issuer or its predecessors or affiliates filed a registration statement that is the subject of a pending proceeding or examination or has been subject to a stop order, has been convicted of any felony or misdemeanor with respect to an SEC filing or has been convicted with respect to any violation of United States Postal Service regulations. Likewise, Regulation A is not available if any director, officer, or general partner of the issuer, any beneficial owner of 10 percent or more of its equity securities, any promoter, any underwriter or any partner, director, or officer of any such underwriter has been convicted of any felony or misdemeanor with respect to securities violations, is subject to a cease and desist order with respect to scienter-based anti-fraud provisions of the securities laws or Section 5 violations, is subject to any order or judgment with respect to securities violations, is suspended or expelled from or barred from association with a member of a national securities exchange or a national

---

[41] 17 C.F.R. §§ 230.251-.263.

securities association or has been convicted with respect to any violation of United States Postal Service regulations.

The Regulation A Bad Boy provisions also apply to issuers relying on Rule 505.

July 10, 2013, the SEC approved new regulations that prohibit issuers from relying on Rule 506 if certain "Bad Boy" provisions apply. The Bad Boy restrictions in Rule 506(d)[42] are substantially similar to those in Regulation A, but not identical. For example, the Regulation A provisions apply to beneficial owners of 10 percent or more of the issuer's outstanding securities, while the Rule 506 provisions only apply to beneficial owners of 20 percent or more.

The Bad Boy restrictions of Rule 506(d) apply to the following "covered persons":

- the issuer and any predecessor of the issuer or affiliated issuer;
- any director, executive officer, other officer participating in the offering, general partner, or managing member of the issuer;
- any beneficial owner of 20 percent or more of the issuer's outstanding securities;
- any investment manager to an issuer that is a pooled investment fund and any director, executive officer, other officer participating in the offering, general partner, or managing member of any such investment manager, as well as any director, executive officer, or officer participating in the offering of any such general partner or managing member;
- any promoter connected with the issuer in any capacity at the time of sale; and
- any person that has been or will be paid direct or indirect remuneration for solicitation of purchasers in connection with sales of the offering and any director, executive officer, other officer participating in the offering, general partner, or managing member of any such compensated solicitor.

---

[42] 17 C.F.R. § 230.506(d).

The issuer cannot rely on Rule 506 if any of the "covered persons":

- Has been convicted, within ten years before such sale (or five years, in the case of issuers, their predecessors, and affiliates), of any felony or misdemeanor:

    o In connection with the purchase or sale of any security;
    o Involving the making of any false filing with the Commission; or
    o Arising out of the conduct of the business of an underwriter, broker, dealer, municipal securities dealer, investment adviser, or paid solicitor of purchasers of securities;

- Is subject to any order, judgment, or decree of any court of competent jurisdiction, entered within five years before such sale, that, at the time of such sale, retrains or enjoins such person from engaging or continuing to engage in any conduct or practice:

    o In connection with the purchase or sale of any security;
    o Involving the making of any false filing with the Commission; or
    o Arising out of the conduct of the business of an underwriter, broker, dealer, municipal securities dealer, investment adviser, or paid solicitor of purchases of securities.

- Is subject to a final order of a state securities commission or similar agency, a state authority that supervises or examines banks, savings associations, or credit unions, a state insurance commission, a federal banking agency, the US Commodity Futures Trading Commission, or the National Credit Union Administration that:

    o At the time of such sale, bars the person from:

        ▪ Association with an entity regulated by such commission, authority, agency, or officer;
        ▪ Engaging in the business of securities, insurance, or banking; or

- ▪ Engaging in savings association or credit union activities; or

  o Constitutes a final order based on a violation of any law or regulation that prohibits fraudulent, manipulative, or deceptive conduct entered within ten years before such sale;

- Is subject to any order of the Commission entered pursuant to Section 15(b) (dealing with broker-dealer registration) or 15B(c) (dealing with brokers, dealers, and municipal securities dealers) of the Securities Exchange Act of 1934[43] or Section 203(e) or (f) of the Investment Advisers Act of 1940[44] that, at the time of such sale:

  o Suspends or revokes such person's registration as a broker, dealer, municipal securities dealer, or investment adviser;
  o Places limitations on the activities, functions, or operations of such person; or
  o Bars such person from being associated with any entity or from participating in the offering of any penny stock;

- Is subject to any order of the Commission entered within five years before such sale that, at the time of such sale, orders the person to cease and desist from committing or causing a violation or future violation of:

  o Any scienter-based anti-fraud provision of the federal securities laws or any other regulation thereunder; or
  o Section 5 of the Securities Act of 1933;[45]

- Is suspended or expelled from membership in, or suspended or barred from association with a member of, a registered national securities exchange or a registered national or affiliated securities association for any conduct inconsistent with just and equitable principles of trade;

---

[43] Securities Exchange Act of 1934, Pub. L. No. 73-291, 48 Stat. 881.
[44] Investment Advisers Act of 1940, 15 U.S.C. §§ 80b-1 to 80b-21.
[45] Securities Act of 1933, Pub. L. No. 73-22, § 5, 48 Stat. 74.

- Have filed, or was named as an underwriter in, and registration statement or Regulation A offering statement filed with the Commission that, within five years before such sale, was the subject of a refusal order, stop order, or order suspending the Regulation A exemption, or is, at the time of such sale, the subject of an investigation or proceeding to determine whether a stop order or suspension order should be issued; or
- Is subject to a United States Postal Service false representation order entered within five years before such sale, or is, at the time of such sale, subject to a temporary restraining order or preliminary injunction with respect to conduct alleged by the United States Postal Service to constitute a scheme or device for obtaining money or property through the mail by means of false representations.

Furthermore, Rule 507 provides that no exemption is available under Rule 504, 505, or 506 for issuers (including predecessors or affiliates) that have been subject to orders, judgments, or decrees of any court that temporarily, preliminarily, or permanently enjoined such issuer for failure to comply with Rule 503 (See Chapter 8 for a discussion about filing Form D).[46]

Information Requirements

Both Rule 505 and 506 require the issuer to comply with all of the information requirements set forth in Rule 502(b)[47] if the offering includes even one unaccredited investor. For these offerings, the issuer will need to prepare written offering materials (typically called an offering memorandum or private placement memorandum) that are substantially similar to a prospectus required for a registered offering, expressly including the following:

- A description of applicable limitations on resale
- If the issuer is not a reporting company, it shall provide:

  o If the issuer is eligible to use Regulation A, the non-financial information that would be required by Part II of Form 1-A. If

---

[46] 17 C.F.R. §§ 230.503-230.507.
[47] *Id.* § 502(b).

the issuer is not eligible to use Regulation A, the non-financial information that would be required by Part I of whatever registration statement the issuer would be eligible to use. Generally, this would include information like the issuer's name, address, date and state of incorporation, phone number, contact people, risk factors of the offering and the issuer, description of the company's business and business plan, description of the issuer's properties and intellectual property, description of the issuer's industry and markets, description of the company's employees, regulatory issues for the issuer, material events, analysis of anticipated profitability timeframe and factors, offering terms like price, minimum and maximum offering, outstanding securities, use of proceeds, anticipated cash flow and liquidity concerns, anticipated future offerings, capitalization, description of securities, plan of distribution, dividends or distributions, information about officers, directors, and other key personnel, current stockholders, management relationships and conflicts of interest, litigation, tax concerns, financial statements, and managements analysis of the issuer's business and future prospects. Disclosure requirements for S-1 registration statements have more requirements than a Regulation A offering document.

o Financial information scaled to the size of the offer as follows:

- Offerings up to $2,000,000--the information required by Article 8 of Regulation S-X, except that only the balance sheet (dated within 120 days of the offering) must be audited.
- Offerings up to $7,500,000--the same financial statements required by Form S-1 for smaller reporting companies. This generally means audited financial statements for at least the two prior years.
- Offerings over $7,500,000--the financial statements that would be required in a registration statement filed under the Securities Act on the form that the issuer would be entitled to use. Generally, this means audited financials for at least two years if the Company qualifies as a "smaller reporting company" and three years if it does not.

- If the issuer is currently a reporting company under Section 13 or 15(d) of the Exchange Act,[48] it shall provide:

  o its most recent proxy statement and Form 10-K;

  o the most recently filed Form 10-K, or a registration statement on S-1, S-11 or Form 10;

  o reports under Section 13(a), 14(a), 14(c), and 15(d) with any information that needs to be updated from the most recent 10-K or registration statement, along with a brief description of the securities being offered, the use of proceeds and any other material changes in the issuer's affairs.

Any document that would be an "exhibit" required to be filed as an exhibit to a registration statement needs to be identified and provided to potential investors upon their request. These "exhibits" generally include governing documents like articles, bylaws, shareholder agreements, voting agreements and the like, material contracts, subsidiaries, plans of acquisition or reorganization, and opinions regarding the legality of the issuance of securities.

Regulation D does not expressly require specific disclosures to accredited investors; however, in view of the antifraud regulations, issuers should provide all prospective investors written materials with the basic information necessary to make an investment decision. At a minimum, this would typically include the terms of the offering and a description of the company, its management and business plan and the use of proceeds of the offering. To the extent available, the issuer should include financial statements for at least the three prior years. Disclosure of significant risk factors or conflicts of interest should also be included. Written disclosures also typically include governance documents such as the articles of incorporation or organization, bylaws, operating agreement, shareholder agreement, investor rights agreement, partnership agreement, or other appropriate agreements.

Providing written information even where not expressly required can benefit the issuer in two ways. First, a well-written disclosure document

---

[48] Securities Exchange Act of 1934, Pub. L. No. 73-291, §§ 13, 15, 48 Stat. 881.

may help sell securities more efficiently by providing prospective investors with the information about the company and the offering they would like to consider in making their investment decision. This can reduce the amount and length of the diligence process. Further, well-written disclosures can help reduce the risk of litigation in the future because the materials ensure that all investors receive consistent thorough written information rather than verbal representations that may be incomplete, inconsistent, misunderstood, or misremembered. If an issuer's business is unsuccessful, disgruntled investors may not recall prior discussions about the risks of investing in the issuer. A well-written disclosure document that clearly sets forth both the risks and benefits of an investment can be critical to the issuer's defense in the face of fraud and misrepresentation allegations.

If the offering under Rule 505 and 506 includes both accredited and unaccredited investors, the same offering materials should be provided to all investors. If information is provided to an accredited investor that is not provided to all unaccredited investors, the issuer should give the unaccredited investors a written description of all information provided to the accredited investors and offer to provide them the same upon request. Likewise, all investors should have the opportunity to ask questions and receive answers concerning the offering and the issuer and the information provided to them.

Integration

If a company conducts multiple offerings within a similar period of time, the Securities and Exchange Commission may consider such offerings in the aggregate for purposes of determining whether they comply with Regulation D or other applicable exemptions. This concept is called "integration." For example, if XYZ conducted one Rule 506 offering with thirty-three unaccredited investors that closed on June 1, 2012 and second Rule 506 offering with twenty-three unaccredited investors that closed on August 1, 2012, the Commission would likely take the position that these offerings should be integrated. As a result, the offerings would not be in compliance with Rule 506 because the integrated offering includes more than thirty-five unaccredited investors and is therefore in violation of Section 5. Integration is also a concern for Rule 504 and Rule 505 offerings as a result of the limitations on the total amount of sales. In the case of Rule 506 offerings to exclusively accredited investors, integration of offerings can be less of a concern because there is no limit on the number of investors or the total amount raised.

In determining whether offerings should be integrated, the Commission considers five factors:

1. Whether the sales are part of a single plan of financing;
2. Whether the sales involve issuance of the same class of securities;
3. Whether the sales have been made at or about the same time;
4. Whether the same type of consideration is being received; and
5. Whether the sales are made for the same general purpose.

In general, the Commission is less likely to determine that two offerings should be integrated if they relate to two different plans of financing, involve different classes and types of securities, if the offerings are separated by time, if the offerings are for different consideration, and if the offerings are for different purposes.

The most critical factor is time. Offers and sales made more than six months prior to the commencement of a Regulation D offering or more than six months after the conclusion of a Regulation D offering will generally not be integrated so long as there are no other sales of similar securities during the gap period. Note that the focus is on "offers and sales" and not just sales. As a result, if XYZ closed one Regulation D offering on February 1, it could not make any offers under a new offering until August 1.

Likewise, offerings made out of the United States in compliance with Regulation S will generally not be integrated with domestic Regulation D offerings. Regulation S of the Securities Act of 1933[49] is an exemption from the Section 5 registration requirements for the sale of securities outside of the United States. There are also certain regulatory safe harbors when considering potential integration between public and

---

[49] 17 C.F.R. §§ 230.901-230.904 (1994).

private offerings. Rule 152[50] provides that a private offering will not generally be integrated with a subsequent public offering that is commenced after completion of the private offering and Rule 155[51] addresses the integration of a failed private offering before a public offering and a failed public offering followed by a private offering.

Determination of whether one or more offerings may be integrated is an inexact science based on the particular facts and circumstances. The Commission has addressed multiple telephone interpretations, other interpretative guidance, and no action letters with a myriad of potential integration scenarios. Any company who plans to offer or sell securities in more than one offering during any six-month period should carefully consider integration issues with their counsel.

The adoption of Rule 506(c)[52] creates some new interesting integration issues for an issuer seeking to conduct a Rule 506(c) offering and a Rule 506(b) (or Rule 505)[53] offering within a similar time frame. Even if all of the other factors suggest that the offerings should not be integrated, a 506(c) offering with advertising and solicitation that takes place immediately before a Rule 506(b) offering (where advertising and solicitation is strictly prohibited) will likely be problematic.

The Commission has indicated that it is considering its policies on integration, particularly in light of Rule 506(c) and other provisions of the JOBS Act. The Commission may issue additional guidance on these issues. Until that time, it is best to separate all Rule 506(c) offerings by at least six months.

Advertising and Solicitation

A key distinction between private offerings and public offerings is the concept that private offerings are between two parties with a pre-existing relationship and therefore, do not include any offering to the public.

---

[50] *Id.* § 230.152.
[51] *Id.* § 230.155.
[52] *Id.* § 230.506(c).
[53] *Id.* § 230.506(b).

Accordingly, advertising and public solicitation of investors have been expressly prohibited for private offerings under Section 4(a)(2), Rule 505, and Rule 506. Advertising and solicitation are also prohibited for offerings under Rule 504 unless offerings are made: (i) exclusively in states that provide for the registration of the securities, including public filing and delivery to investors of a substantial disclosure document before sale; (ii) in states that do not require the registration of the securities, provided that the securities are registered in another state that does have such a requirement; or (iii) sold exclusively according to state law exemptions that permit general solicitation and general advertising so long as all sales are to accredited investors. This restriction has been interpreted broadly to prohibit a wide range of solicitation activities including mass e-mails or other written correspondence, phone banks, websites and other offers of securities to large groups. SEC guidance has indicated that in a private offering, solicitations may only be made to investors with whom the issuer, its officers and directors or placement agent have a pre-existing business or personal relationship.

These prohibitions on advertising and solicitation can make it more difficult for issuers to raise money in a private offering because it can be a challenge for issuers to identify potential investors from their own pool of personal contacts. Using registered brokers or placement agents with a wide range of contacts can help identify suitable investors from a wider pool, but adds additional costs to the offering.

The JOBs Act has put a new spin on this historic restriction. On July 10, 2013, the SEC issued Release 33-9415 which adopted amendments to Regulation D permitting public solicitation and advertising for certain Regulation D Rule 506 offerings. The Release creates a new subsection Rule 506(c) permitting advertising and solicitation provided that: (i) all other conditions of Rule 506 are met; (ii) all investors are accredited; and (iii) the issuer takes additional steps to verify the accredited status of the investors. The steps required for verification are discussed in detail below, but in general, issuers seeking to rely on Rule 506(c) must perform more diligence to confirm the accredited status of their investors; merely asking investors to check a box in the subscription agreement is not adequate.

Marketing opportunities for Rule 506(c) offerings are significantly more expansive. Issuers can approach investors with whom they do not have any pre-existing relationship. They can advertise, engage in mass solicitations and provide information about their offerings on a website.

Before engaging in a Rule 506(c) offering, issuers should consider whether they are willing to perform the enhanced diligence process to determine the accredited status of their investors. This diligence process may be more expensive and time-consuming than traditional diligence because it entails an affirmative obligation to review documents confirming the investor's financial condition. Further, some investors may find this enhanced diligence to be invasive and may be unwilling to participate in 506(c) offerings.

In addition, all information provided in a private offering whether provided pursuant to a private offering memorandum or public advertising remains subject to state and federal anti-fraud laws.

While there is little precedent on the scope of the SEC's review of advertising and solicitation materials for Rule 506(c) offerings, existing guidance for registration statements and prospectuses and solicitation materials for brokers should provide a good road map. For example, SEC Rule 206(4)-1[54] and related guidance govern advertising for investment advisers, including acceptable forms of performance advertising. Performance advertising typically receives enhanced regulatory scrutiny. Issuers that plan to use advertising materials should keep these guidelines in mind. General advertisements that refer potential investors who have established their accredited status to more detailed offering materials are likely to be less problematic than advertisements that promise great returns. Sometimes these are called tombstone ads.

The anti-fraud regulations apply to all information provided to investors, so issuers should carefully review their materials to make sure they provide accurate and complete information about the company and the offering.

---

[54] 17 C.F.R. § 275.206(4)-1

Limitations on Resale

Securities sold pursuant to Regulation D Rule 506 are considered "restricted securities" which means they cannot be resold without registration under the Act or the availability of some other exemption. Securities sold under Regulation D typically have a legend alerting the holder to this restricted status. A typical restricted security legend will read something like this:

> The shares represented by this certificate have not been registered under the Securities Act of 1933, as amended, or the securities laws of any state. Accordingly, these shares may not be sold, hypothecated, pledged or otherwise transferred except (i) pursuant to an effective registration statement under the Securities Act of 1933, as amended, and any applicable securities laws or regulations of any state with respect to such shares, (ii) in accordance with Securities and Exchange Commission Rule 144, or (iii) upon the issuance to the Company of a favorable opinion of counsel or the submission to the Company of such other evidence as may be satisfactory to the Company that such proposed sale, assignment, encumbrance or other transfer will not be in violation of the Securities Act of 1933, as amended, or any applicable securities laws of any state or any rules or regulations thereunder. Any attempted transfer of this certificate or the shares represented hereby which is in violation of the preceding restrictions will not be recognized by the Company, nor will any transferee be recognized as the owner thereof by the Company.

To ensure their future ability to sell the restricted securities, purchasers of private placement securities may negotiate registration rights. Typically, these registration rights will provide that if the issuer files a registration statement at some point in the future, the investors will have the right to require the issuer to file a registration statement to register the private placement shares as well. These are called "piggy back registration rights." Sometimes, the registration rights will allow the holders to demand registration at any time. These are called "demand registration rights." The terms and conditions are set forth in a Registration Rights Agreement that describes when the obligation to register private placement shares might arise. Registration rights are more common in public companies or companies with imminent plans to go public.

In the absence of the subsequent registration of the restricted shares, investors in private placement offerings typically rely on Rule 144 with respect to the resale of their shares. Rule 144 provides that if the applicable conditions are met, the seller will not be deemed to be engaged in a distribution and will not therefore be considered an underwriter as defined in Section 2(a)(11) for purposes of eligibility for the exemption under Section 4(a)(1).[55] Rule 144 basically requires security holders to demonstrate their intent to hold the securities and not to merely act as a reseller by meeting certain holding period requirements. Security holders may resell their restricted securities after a six-month holding period if the issuer has: (i) filed all required reports under Section 13 or 15(d) during the preceding twelve months; (ii) been subject to filing requirements for at least ninety days; and (iii) has submitted and posted every Interactive Date File required by Rule 405 of Regulation S-T[56] during the preceding twelve months. If the issuer is not a public company and has not complied with such public reporting requirements, security holders must hold the securities at least one year. Affiliates may also be subject to volume limitations and public notice filing on Form 144.

Verification of Accredited Status

Historically, issuers verified the accredited status of prospective investors by having the investors execute a subscription agreement making representations about their accredited status. Further, issuers had to reasonably believe that the investor was accredited and the issuer could not be aware of any information suggesting otherwise. Since, in theory, the issuer and investors had a pre-existing relationship, the issuer should have had reason to know whether each investor was accredited, so their belief in conjunction with the investor's representations was generally considered adequate.

---

[55] Securities Act of 1933, Pub. L. No. 73-22, §§ 2(A)(11), 4(a)(1), 48 Stat. 74.
[56] 17 C.F.R. § 230.405.

The final rules for 506(c) offerings make clear that merely asking investors to "check the box" in a subscription agreement to confirm their accredited status is not sufficient for 506(c) offerings. Rather, issuers must take "reasonable" steps to confirm accredited status, which is dependent on the:

- Nature of the purchaser and type of accredited investor the purchaser claims to be;
- Amount and type of information the issuer has about the purchaser; and
- Nature of the offering, such as the manner in which the purchaser was solicited and the terms of the offering, including the minimum offering amount.

For example, if the purchaser is accredited as a result of their status as a registered broker-dealer or investment company, the issuer can verify this registration status through public sources. Likewise, if the purchaser is an executive officer of a publicly registered company, a famous athlete or another type of public figure whose salary or net worth is publicly available from reliable sources, this information may be sufficient to verify accredited status. The purchaser's ability to meet a significant minimum investment for the offering (in excess of $1,000,000) may be another relevant factor in determining that the purchaser has a net worth sufficient to establish accredited status. While these suggestions are very helpful when considering certain types of investors, most offerings have lesser minimum purchase prices and involve purchasers whose incomes are not publicly disclosed. Verification of these individuals is more difficult, so the SEC recommends four non-exclusive verification methods:

1. *Tax Returns*--a purchaser who claims accredited status based on his or her income can provide the issuer copies of their Form W-2, Form 1099, Schedule K-1, and Form 1040, as applicable, for the two most recent years, along with a written representation that they anticipate reaching the required income level in the current year.

2. *Verification of Assets and Liabilities*--a purchaser who claims accredited status based on his or her net worth can provide the issuer with bank statements, brokerage statements, certificates of

deposit, tax assessments, and appraisal reports to establish their assets. The purchaser's liabilities may be established by a credit report and a written representation from the purchaser as to all of his or her liabilities.

3. *Confirmation Letter*--in lieu of presenting tax or account statement information to the issuer, a purchaser can obtain written confirmation of his or her accredited status from a registered broker-dealer, SEC registered investment adviser, licensed attorney, or certified public accountant confirming that such person has taken reasonable steps (such as reviewing tax forms, bank statements, etc.) to confirm that purchaser's accredited status within the prior three months.

4. *Prior Accreditation*--Accredited investors who invested in an issuer's Rule 506(b) offering conducted prior to July 10, 2013 who remain an investor will continue to be considered accredited investors for the purposes of subsequent Rule 506(c) offerings conducted by the same issuer, provided that the investor provides a certificate confirming their accredited status.[57]

None of these verifications methods will be deemed "reasonable" if the issuer has knowledge that the purchaser is not accredited.

The increased diligence requirement for Rule 506(c) offerings can be a challenge because many investors will not be comfortable providing their tax returns or other account statements to issuers, especially issuers with whom they have no pre-existing relationship. Investors have expressed legitimate privacy and identity theft concerns. It is likely that investors who regularly invest in private offerings will have a confirmation letter prepared by their attorney, accountant, investment adviser, or other appropriate party who is already familiar with their financial status. Other more sporadic accredited investors may be unwilling to participate in Rule 506(c) offerings out of concern for providing this confidential information.

Offerings conducted pursuant to Regulation D exemptions other than Rule 506(c) are not currently required to comply with these enhanced verification procedures. However, some issuers may choose to follow these procedures to provide additional assurance that all investors in their offering have satisfied the requirements to be an accredited investor.

6

Regulation D Exemption Alternatives

Regulation D provides three exemption alternatives with slightly different limits and conditions. The advantages and disadvantages of each alternative are summarized below.

Rule 504

The exemption provided by Rule 504 exempts offerings of up to $1,000,000 of securities during any rolling twelve-month period. This $1,000,000 limit is reduced by any other offerings conducted during the previous twelve months, the exemption provided by Section 3(b), or in violation of Section 5(a) of the Exchange Act.[58] Rule 504 is not available to public companies, investment companies, or certain development stage companies.

No general solicitation or advertising is permitted and securities are generally considered Restricted Securities subject to resale limitations. Resale limitations and solicitation and advertising prohibitions do not apply if the securities are offered and sold: (i) exclusively in one or more states that require the registration of the securities and public filing and delivery of a substantial disclosure document to investors prior to purchase; (ii) in one or more states that do not require registration of the securities, provided that the securities have been registered in at least one other state and that the disclosure document required therein is provided to all investors prior to purchase; or (iii) exclusively pursuant to state exemptions from registration

---

[58] Securities Exchange Act of 1934, Pub. L. No. 73-291, §§ 3(b), 5, 48 Stat. 881.

that permit general solicitation and advertising so long as sales are made only to accredited investors.

Rule 505

Rule 505 exempts offerings of up to $5,000,000 of securities during any rolling twelve-month period to up to thirty-five unaccredited purchasers and an unlimited number of accredited investors. Rule 505 offerings are subject to all of the conditions of Rule 502[59] including integration, information requirements, the prohibition on solicitation and advertising, and limitations on resale.

Rule 501(e)[60] indicates that when counting the number of purchasers, the following may be excluded: (i) any relative or spouse of a purchaser with the same primary residence; (ii) any trust or estate in which a purchaser owns more than 50 percent of the beneficial interests (excluding contingent interests); (iii) any corporation or other organization in which a purchaser owns more than 50 percent of the equity interests; and (iv) accredited investors. Accordingly, if Bob buys fifty shares of XYZ Inc. in his own name, fifty shares in the name of his minor daughter Bobbi, fifty shares in the name of Bob Inc. (Bob owns 85 percent of the issued and outstanding Bob Inc. stock), and fifty shares by the Bob Revocable Trust (where Bob, his wife Roberta and daughter Bobbi are the sole beneficiaries), all 200 shares purchased only count as one purchaser for purposes of the thirty-five purchaser limit. If Bob is an accredited investor, neither Bob, Bob Inc., Bobbi or the Bob Revocable Trust would count as a purchaser for purposes of the calculating the unaccredited investor limit.

Issuers disqualified by the Regulation A "Bad Boy" restrictions, as described above in Chapter 5, are not eligible to rely on Rule 505.

Rule 506—The Prom King of Regulation D Exemptions

Rule 506 is the most popular Regulation D exemption for two reasons. First, Rule 506 exempts sales of an unlimited amount of securities to up

---

[59] 17 C.F.R. § 230.502.
[60] *Id.* § 230.501(e).

to thirty-five sophisticated unaccredited purchasers and an unlimited number of sophisticated accredited investors. The ability to offer an unlimited amount to an unlimited number of accredited investors makes it the preferred choice for private offerings by hedge funds, private equity funds, and other issuers seeking to sell large amounts. Often, at the beginning of an offering, an issuer may not know exactly how many investors will be interested in participating, which makes the flexibility of Rule 506 even more attractive. All Rule 506 investors must be sophisticated or have a sophisticated purchaser representative (see Chapter 4 for a discussion of the sophistication requirement).

The second reason for the popularity of Rule 506 is that securities sold under Rule 506 are considered "Covered Securities" for state securities law compliance purposes. As discussed in more detail in Chapter 7, this means states cannot require state registration of Rule 506 offerings. States can require issuers to file a copy of the same Form D filed with the SEC along with a filing fee. As a result, Rule 506 offerings are generally much simpler to conduct than Rule 504 or Rule 505 offerings, especially where investors reside in multiple states.

Rule 506(b),[61] the OE (original exemption) of Regulation D

Rule 506(b) offerings are subject to all of the conditions of Section 502 including integration, information requirements, and limitations on resale. Rule 506(b) offerings also prohibit all advertising and solicitation. Following the adoption of Rule 506(c), traditional Rule 506 offerings became known as "Rule 506(b)." Issuers conducting Rule 506(b) offerings can verify the accreditation of their investors through traditional means, including a subscription agreement with appropriate investor representations. Rule 506(b) offerings permit up to thirty-five non-accredited investors, although inclusion of even one non-accredited investor requires compliance with enhanced disclosure requirements (see the discussion in Chapter 5).

So long as all offerees and purchasers are accredited, issuers can sell an unlimited number of securities to an unlimited number of investors with no express disclosure obligations. However, most issuers conducting Rule 506

---

[61] 17 C.F.R. § 230.506.

offerings to all accredited investors will prepare some type of disclosure document (often called an "offering memorandum" or "private placement memorandum") that sets forth the salient terms of the offering, describes the company and its business plan and provides some basic financial statement information (to the extent such information exists).

New Rule 506(c)

In July of 2013, the SEC adopted amendments to Regulation D that permit advertising and solicitation for offerings conducted pursuant to the newly created Rule 506(c).[62] This rule proposal was mandated by the JOBs Act and is highly controversial. While many in the investment community believe that allowing solicitation and advertising will greatly improve the ability of small early stage issuers to raise capital, others worry that advertising and solicitation will make it easier for fraudsters to take advantage of unwary investors. All advertising and solicitation remains subject to the anti-fraud provisions in state and federal securities laws, but regulatory agencies do not have the resources to identify and monitor all questionable offerings.

Rule 506(c) allows advertising and solicitation provided that all of the investors are accredited and that the issuer has taken enhanced steps to verify the accreditation status of the investors. As discussed in Chapter 5, merely checking "accredited" on a subscription agreement is not an adequate amount of diligence. Issuers considering engaging in Rule 506(c) offerings should consider whether they are willing to perform the enhanced diligence and whether their prospective investors will be willing to provide the required documentation.

Offerings pursuant to Rule 506(c) present some unique risks to issuers. First, issuers must perform a sufficient amount of diligence to determine that all investors are accredited. Failure to take adequate steps to confirm this status could result in a loss of the exemption and a violation of Section 5 if an unaccredited investor participates in the offering. Second, the advertising materials themselves may be a source of liability if investors or regulatory agencies believe they are misleading, inaccurate or omit critical

---

[62] 17 C.F.R. § 230.506(c).

information. Since at least some of these materials are public, they may receive more regulatory scrutiny than materials prepared for traditional private offerings.

Issuers can protect themselves by limiting advertising to basic information and then providing a more fulsome disclosure document to prospective investors that have established their accredited status. Issuers should also avoid representations about the performance of the security in advertisements where the underlying assumptions cannot be fully explained. For example, this type of advertisement would likely be heavily scrutinized:

"Invest in XYZ Inc. common stock and double your investment in two years!"

The statement alone promises a huge return but does not include any information about the likelihood of achieving this return, the risk factors or the other circumstances that would be necessary to achieve this type of return.

In contrast, issuers might consider this type of tombstone advertising:

"XYZ Inc., manufacturer of the SuperZ Widget, is conducting an offering of up to $5,000,000 of common stock to accredited investors only. For more information, please contact Buford T. Xenon, President of XYZ."

This statement provides only general information about the issuer and the offering. Qualified interested investors will then receive a disclosure packet containing all of the relevant information about the company and the offering.

When to Use Reg D versus Other Exemption Alternatives

There are other exemptions from registration that issuers may be able to utilize that may be preferable to Regulation D in certain circumstances.

Regulation S

Regulation S exempts offerings to investors who reside overseas from US registration requirements, although such offerings may be subject to regulatory provisions in the jurisdiction where the investors reside. If the prospective investors in your offering reside out of the United States, Regulation S is a viable alternative. There is no filing required for Regulation S compliance but the issuer should take care to confirm the residence of each investor and confirm compliance with any applicable foreign securities laws. Regulation S offerings can be conducted at the same time as Regulation D offerings without integration concerns. For example, XYZ Inc. could sell 1,500 shares of common stock to three investors residing in Germany, Brazil, and Australia pursuant to Regulation S. At the same time, XYZ Inc. could conduct a Rule 506(b)[63] offering in the United States to up to thirty-five non-accredited investors or an unlimited number of accredited investors.

Regulation A

Regulation A provides a "mini-registration" process for offerings. Historically, issuers could sell up to $5,000,000 in a twelve-month period pursuant to Regulation A, but newly approved amendments pursuant to the JOBs Act increased this limit to $20,000,000 for Tier I offerings and $50,000,000 for Tier II offerings. Issuers are required to file the Form 1-A registration statement with the Commission prior to commencing any offering and Form 1-A must be provided to prospective investors prior to investing in the offering. Regulation A offerings are considered public offerings, so there is no prohibition on general solicitation and advertising. Likewise, Regulation A securities are not considered "restricted" and subject to resale limitations. Regulation A Tier II issuers are subject to additional disclosure and ongoing reporting requirements.

Regulation A has not been frequently used because of the obligation to file the Form 1-A with the SEC in advance and because securities sold under Regulation A are not considered Covered Securities and are therefore subject to state registration requirements. Under the newly adopted amendments, securities sold pursuant to Tier II will be considered covered securities. For example, in 2012 there were only eight qualified Regulation A offerings for $34.5 million compared to approximately 7,700 Regulation D offerings up to $5,000,000 for $7

---

[63] 17 C.F.R. § 230.506(b).

billion.[64] It is possible that the revisions to Regulation A (often called Regulation A+) will make it a more attractive alternative for issuers seeking to conduct an offering.

Regulation A may be a good alternative for offerings conducted within a small number of states where the issuer would like to use advertising and solicitation, but does not want to restrict the offering to accredited investors. Many states have registration requirements for Regulation A offerings that require similar information to the Form 1-A filed with the Securities and Exchange Commission that can help make the process more efficient.

Crowdfunding

Another exemption alternative that has recently received a lot of press is crowdfunding. The term "crowdfunding" is frequently misused and can be a source of confusion for prospective issuers and investors. Sometimes, the media uses the term "crowdfunding" to refer to any type of offering involving the general solicitation of investors, including registered offerings, Regulation A, and Regulation D offerings. "Crowdfunding" is also sometimes used to describe fundraising where issuers or others ask for donations with no stock or other remuneration given to the donors. For purposes of this discussion (and as far as the SEC is concerned), "crowdfunding" refers only to the exemption available through Section 4(a)(6) of the JOBSs Act[65] which exempts offerings up to $1,000,000 during any twelve-month period.

Pursuant to Section 4(a)(6), sales to individual investors under all Section 4(a)(6) crowdfunding offerings (not just the issuer's offering) cannot exceed the higher of: (a) if either annual income or net worth is greater than $100,000, the greater of 10 percent of (i) annual income or (ii) net worth up to $100,000; or (b) if neither annual income nor net worth exceed $100,000, the greater of $2,000 or 5 percent of annual income or net worth. Only private domestic companies will be permitted to conduct crowdfunding offerings.

---

[64] Proposed Rule Amendments for Small and Additional Issues Exemptions under Section 3(b) of the Securities Act, Release No 33-9497, p. 11 (Dec. 18, 2013).

[65] Jumpstart Our Business Startups Act, Pub. L. No. 112-106, § 4(a)(6), 126 Stat. 306 (2012).

Sales will be conducted through online funding portals managed by intermediaries registered with the SEC. Issuers are required to disclose certain information about their operations and the offerings, although the disclosure requirements are significantly less burdensome than a prospectus for a registered offering. Disclosure items include items such as:

- Name, address, website, and legal status of the issuer
- Names of officers, directors, and shareholders owning more than 20 percent of the issuer
- Description of the business and its business plan
- Description of the financial condition of the issuer
- Anticipated use of proceeds of funds raised
- Targeted offering amount and timeline of the offering
- Price of the securities and how the price was determined
- Description of the capital structure

Section 4(a)(6) will go into effect upon adoption of final regulations by the SEC. Regulations were proposed in October of 2013, but to date, have not been finalized. Accordingly, crowdfunding (at least the kind contemplated by the JOBS Act) remains illegal for federal purposes at this time.

Many states have undertaken crowdfunding legislation to create intrastate crowdfunding exemptions. Some of these exemptions parallel the limits and disclosure requirements contemplated by Section 4(a)(6) while others adopt different requirements. For example, in April 2015, Colorado adopted the Colorado Crowdfunding Act,[66] which provides for intrastate crowdfunding offerings of up to $1,000,000 (or $2,000,000 if the issuer has audited financial statements. All investors and the issuer must reside in Colorado (or be organized in Colorado) and at least 80 percent of the proceeds of the offering must be used in Colorado. Offerings must be conducted through registered online intermediaries, and are subject to disclosure requirements, limits on the amounts invested, ongoing reporting obligations and other requirements set forth in the statute and contemplated regulations.

---

[66] COLO. REV. STAT. § 11-51-308.5

This is a rapidly evolving area of legislation, so if you are considering structuring a crowdfunding offering, you should confirm the status of applicable state and federal legislation to determine which exemptions may be available to you.

Representatives of the SEC, state regulatory agencies and other investor protection organizations have expressed a number of concerns about crowdfunding. Their chief concern is that unaccredited unsophisticated investors with limited financial means will be targeted by issuers selling interests in risky early stage ventures. These investors may not be capable of adequately analyzing the risk of the investment or bearing the loss of all of their funds. Proponents of crowdfunding argue that it will give small startup ventures an easier more cost-effective way to raise funds and that investors are protected by mandatory disclosure requirements and significant limitations on the amounts that can be invested. Some SEC representatives have indicated that they would like the final rules to include additional investor protections while proponents of crowdfunding argue that crowdfunding is only useful if it is an easy, inexpensive, efficient process.

Until the final federal crowdfunding regulations are adopted, it is impossible to know whether crowdfunding will become a significant method for raising capital or whether issuers and investors prefer to stick with Regulation D and other offerings that are more familiar.

Which Reg D Provision Is Best for Different Situations

As mentioned above, Rule 506 is the most commonly used exemption under Regulation D for three reasons. First, Rule 506 allows sales to an unlimited number of accredited investors with no dollar cap so it provides the most flexibility. Second, securities sold pursuant to Rule 506 are also "Covered Securities" under the PSLRA and are therefore subject to limited state regulation (See Chapter 7 for a more in-depth review of blue sky issues). Finally, Rule 506 offerings solely to accredited investors do not have express disclosure requirements, although issuers remain obligated to provide sufficient information necessary for investors to evaluate the investment opportunity. Issuers conducting Rule 506 offerings exclusively to accredited investors also have the option of using advertising and solicitation pursuant to Rule 506(c).

The biggest disadvantage to Rule 506 is that the securities sold in such offerings are considered restricted and cannot be immediately resold. In addition, Rule 506 offerings that include even one unaccredited investor are subject to disclosure requirements substantially similar to a prospectus and a limitation of thirty-five unaccredited investors.

While Rule 506 is the most commonly used Form D exemption, there are situations where Rule 504 or Rule 505 may make more sense. For example, if the issuer or any of its covered persons are subject to a disqualifying "Bad Boy" event under Rule 505 or Rule 506, the issuer may still be able to conduct an offering under Rule 504. If the offering includes accredited investors who are not sophisticated, Rule 505 could be preferable.

Likewise, if the offering is for less than $1,000,000 and will include unaccredited investors located in states with applicable small offering exemptions, Rule 504 may be preferable because there are no express federal disclosure requirements, although state law may impose disclosure obligations.

Battle Royale: 506(b) versus 506(c)

As discussed in the prior section, historically, most issuers have preferred Rule 506 over other exemption alternatives. Following the recent enactment of regulations authorizing Rule 506(c), issuers opting to use Rule 506 must now consider whether to conduct offerings under Rule 506(b) or Rule 506(c). Before commencing the offering, issuers should carefully consider whether the potential benefits of advertising or solicitation are worth the additional expense and risk inherent in Rule 506(c) offerings.

If an issuer anticipates that its offering may include even one unaccredited investor, it should structure the offering pursuant to Section 506(b) and avoid any advertising or solicitation. If an issuer is not sure how an offering will progress, it should start the offering as Rule 506(b) offering to exclusively accredited investors. If necessary (assuming the offering has been to solely accredited investors), the issuer can convert to a Rule 506(c) offering later. Once an issuer has engaged in advertising and solicitation, the offering cannot be converted to a Rule 506(b) offering. Likewise, if a Rule 506(b) offering includes even one unaccredited investor, it cannot be converted to Rule 506(c) offering.

When contemplating both a Rule 506(b) offering to unaccredited investors and a Rule 506(c) offering with advertising and solicitation, the issuer and its counsel should carefully consider the integration rules discussed in Chapter 5. To avoid integration concerns, these offerings should be distinct and at least six months apart.

7

NSMIA and Blue Sky Compliance

In addition to complying with all applicable federal laws and Securities and Exchange Commission regulations and guidance concerning private offerings, issuers will also need to consider applicable state laws and regulations. Each state has its own regulatory scheme for offerings to its residents. State securities regulations are often called "blue sky." Historically, these regulations varied widely from state to state, making it difficult and time-consuming to conduct private offerings to citizens of multiple states.

In 1996, Congress passed the National Securities Markets Improvements Act of 1996[67] to improve efficiency and promote capital formation in the capital markets by limiting the scope of state regulation for certain offerings. The Act, commonly known as "NSMIA," prohibited states from requiring the registration or qualification of "Covered Securities." With respect to offerings of Covered Securities, states are permitted to impose notice filing requirements that are substantially similar to notice filing requirements required by the SEC and states may enforce their anti-fraud regulations.

The definition of Covered Securities includes securities sold pursuant to Section 4(a)(2) or regulations adopted thereunder. Rule 506 was adopted pursuant to Section 4(a)(2) while Rules 504 and 505 were adopted pursuant to the authority in Section 3(b) of the Securities Act. Accordingly, securities

---

[67] National Securities Markets Improvements Act of 1996, Pub. L. No. 104-290, 110 Stat. 3416.

sold pursuant to Rule 506 are considered "covered securities" while securities sold pursuant to Rule 504 and 505 are not.

The practical impact of NSMIA is that most states have an exemption for Regulation D Rule 506 offerings that requires filing of the Form D within fifteen days of the first sale along with a filing fee. Filing fees vary, but are typically in the $50 to $500 range. Some states require a manual signature on the Form D and some states request certain information in the cover letter such as the date of the first sale or number of investors in that state. In addition, some states have adopted electronic filing through EFD as discussed in Chapter 8. Issuers should confirm the applicable filing requirements with their counsel.

Many states also have other exemptions for private offerings that may apply, such as offerings to a limited number of investors (usually less than fifteen) or offerings to exclusively accredited investors. These exemptions may be self-executing, which means that there is no notice filing or fee required.

Most states also have broker-dealer registration requirements that require anyone selling securities to register as a broker; however, many states have exemptions to these requirements for officers of the issuer who assist with sales of securities, provided the officers do not receive any express compensation tied to the sales.

Similar to federal law, most states require either registration of offerings or compliance with a registration exemption. New York's Martin Act[68] takes a unique approach to regulation of offerings. Rather than requiring registration or exemption from registration for offerings, the Martin Act requires issuers and their representatives to register as dealers before effecting the sale of their own securities to the public. This regulatory scheme does not easily reconcile with NSMIA. Many practitioners have taken the position that the Martin Act is preempted by NSMIA and therefore offerings of Covered Securities pursuant to Regulation D Rule 506 are not subject to the Martin Act requirements. In 2002, the Committee on Securities Regulation of the Business Law Section of the

---

[68] N.Y. GEN. BUS. LAW §§ 352-353.

New York State Bar Association issued a position paper explaining this position. The position paper was submitted to the New York State Attorney General but was never formally accepted or rejected.

The Martin Act only applies to "offers for sale to the public" but that term is not clearly defined. There is some question whether the Martin Act would apply to offerings pursuant to Regulation D Rule 506(c) since such offerings may include advertising and solicitation. Most practitioners have taken the position that Rule 506(c) offerings should be treated the same as Rule 506(b) offerings, but the New York Investor Protection Bureau may not agree with that analysis.

If you contemplate offering any securities to New York residents, you should check with your counsel first to determine whether any pre-filings are necessary before commencing the offering.

If you anticipate that any of your investors will reside outside of the United States, the sale of securities to such international investors may be exempt under either Regulation D or Regulation S for United States regulatory purposes, but may be subject to regulatory requirements of the investor's home country.

Accordingly, it is critical for you to consult with knowledgeable securities counsel before commencing a private placement offering to ensure that you are in compliance with all applicable state and federal laws.

8

Form D and Filing Procedures

Pursuant to Rule 503,[69] issuers relying on Regulation D must file Form D with the SEC no later than fifteen calendar days after the first sale of securities in the offering (unless that date is a Saturday, Sunday, or holiday, in which case the deadline is the first business day thereafter). The first closing is the date the issuer first accepts funds and subscription agreements from investors. Form D must be filed electronically with the SEC and upon filing, it can be viewed on the SEC website.

As described further below, Form D may also be required in the states where investors reside. Many state securities commissions have been working with the National Association of Securities Administrations Association (NASAA) to develop an electronic filing mechanism for state compliance. NASAA is a national organization comprised primarily of state securities agencies. This system finally got up and running at the end of 2014 allowing investors to make one electronic filing covering multiple participating states for Rule 506 offerings.

SEC Filing Codes

Before an issuer can file Form D electronically with the SEC, it must have "filing codes" to enter the EDGAR filing system. To obtain filing codes, the issuer should go to the EDGAR Filer Management website at www.filermanagement.edgarfiling.sec.gov and click the link for "Apply for EDGAR Access." This link will bring up a short form called "Apply for EDGAR Access (New)" that asks for basic information about issuer including the issuer's:

---

[69] 17 C.F.R. §§ 230.503.

- name
- address
- phone number
- Tax Identification Number
- state of incorporation
- fiscal year end
- contact name and information for questions about EDGAR (usually the lawyer handling the filing)
- contact name and information for questions about the SEC account (usually the CEO, President, or other officer who is handling the filings)
- signature for the officer or other person who is duly authorized to sign on behalf of the issuer.

After filling out the electronic form, it should be printed and manually signed by the authorized signatory (sign next to the electronic signature) and then notarized. The manually signed and notarized copy should be saved as a pdf file and uploaded to the electronic submission of the Application for EDGAR Access.

As part of the application, the submitter will need to come up with a Passphrase. After submitting the electronic application, the person identified as the SEC Contact person will receive an e-mail back from the SEC with confirmation that the application was either accepted or rejected. If the application was accepted, the e-mail will contain a CIK code for the issuer.

To complete the application process, click on the link in the e-mail to the SEC Filer Management page and click on "Generate Access Codes (New/Replacement)" and submit the CIK Code and Passphrase. This will generate the following EDGAR Access Codes: CIK, Password, CCC, and PMAC. It is very important to save these codes, along with the Passphrase, as they will be necessary for any future SEC filings.

The process for obtaining filing codes can take a couple days, so you should commence this process well in advance of the fifteen-day deadline for filing the Form D. You can obtain filing codes prior to closing to make sure you are able to timely submit your Form D.

SEC Filing of Form D

Form D asks for basic information about the issuer and the offering. You can print out a copy of Form D here: https://www.sec.gov/about/forms/formd.pdf, but remember that the actually filing will need to be made by filling out the blanks on the electronic submission.

The information required by Form D includes the following:

- name
- address
- year of incorporation
- state of incorporation
- type of entity
- CIK
- Name, address, and position of all "Related Persons." Related Persons include people with management control such as executive officers, directors, promoters, general and managing partners, and managing members.
- Industry group
- Issuer size (based on revenues, unless issuer is a fund, then based on aggregate net asset value range)
- Exemption applied for
- Duration of offering (more or less than one year)
- Type of securities offered
- Is offering in connection with a business combination?
- Minimum investment from any investor
- The name, address, and CRD number of anyone receiving sales compensation in connection with the offering and the states in which they offered securities
- Total dollar amount of the offering and amount sold to date
- Number of investors in the offering and the number of unaccredited investors
- Sales commissions and finders fees paid
- Amount, if any, of the proceeds proposed to be used for payments to the executive officers, directors or promoters listed as Related Persons.

When the issuer is ready to file Form D, it will log into the SEC EDGAR portal[70] using its filing codes. Form D will be signed electronically for submission to the Commission, but should also be printed out and manually signed by the responsible officer. The manually signed Form D should be maintained in the issuer's records. In addition, some states require a manually executed Form D (see Chapter 7). There is no filing fee for the SEC filing, but most states do require a filing fee.

State Filing of Form D

In December 2014, NASAA and various state securities regulatory agencies announced the launch of an online Electronic Filing Depository (EFD) for Rule 506 offerings. The system will allow issuers to submit a copy of Form D, as filed with the SEC, to multiple state securities regulators and pay applicable state fees through the EFD website. The EFD has been in the works for several years and many states actually had statutes mandating electronic filing of Form D before the system was in operation.

The SEC electronic filing must be made first, and then EFD will link to it through the SEC accession number. The accession number is an identifying number assigned by the SEC to the Form D at the time the Form D is filed.

To make filings through EFD, issuers will need to set up an account in advance. Detailed instructions about the registration process are available on the EFD website at www.efdnasaa.org if you click on "GET STARTED" and then "MORE DETAILS."

A list of states participating in EFD is available at https://www.efdnasaa.org/About. For non-participating states, the issuer will still need to submit a paper copy of Form D along with any required filing fee.

NASAA plans to expand the use of the EFD to including regulatory filings for other types of offerings in the future.

---

[70] *Electronic Data Gathering, Analysis, and Retrieval (EDGAR)*, U.S. SECURITIES & EXCHANGE COMMISSION, http://www.portal.edgarfiling.sec.gov/Welcome/EDGARPortal.htm.

Before commencing your offering, you should confirm with your counsel whether electronic Form D filings with the states where your investors reside are permitted, mandatory, or non-available.

9

Very, Very Bad Things: Regulatory and Litigation Pitfalls

Issuers conducting private placement offerings have three different sources of potential liability related to the offering. First, the company could face private claims from investors under state or federal law alleging statutory fraud, securities fraud, common law fraud, breach of contract, or fraud in the inducement. These claims usually result from allegations that the issuer or its representatives provided incomplete or inaccurate information to the investors. Existing owners of the issuer could make claims for breach of fiduciary duties or breach of contract if the new offering was contrary to the best interests of the issuer or breached provisions of a shareholder agreement, investors rights, or other similar agreement.

Second, the issuer could face an enforcement action from the SEC. Most private offering federal investigations allege: (i) the offering was conducted without registration or compliance with an appropriate exemption from registration and/or (ii) the investors to the offering were misled or defrauded pursuant to Rule 10b-5[71] promulgated under of the Securities Exchange Act. 10b-5, as it is known, is a broad prohibition on deceptive conduct that applies to any deceptive or fraudulent act related to the purchase or sale of any security. It reads:

> It shall be unlawful for any person, directly or indirectly, by the use of any means or instrumentality of interstate commerce, or of the mails or of any facility of any national securities exchange,

---

[71] 17 C.F.R. § 240.10b-5.

(a) To employ any device, scheme, or artifice to defraud,

(b) To make any untrue statement of a material fact or to omit to state a material fact necessary in order to make the statements made, in the light of the circumstances under which they were made, not misleading, or

(c) To engage in any act, practice, or course of business which operates or would operate as a fraud or deceit upon any person, in connection with the purchase or sale of any security

If a plaintiff can establish actual damages caused by a misstatement or omission pursuant to Section 10(b), it may receive its out-of-pocket damages. In addition, the SEC may impose civil money penalties for each violation up to $100,000 for natural persons or $500,000 for entities. Criminal penalties may include fines, disgorgement, or up to five years of imprisonment. Sanctions may also include injunctions or cease-and-desist orders. Individuals responsible for the fraudulent activity may also be subject to bar orders that prevent them from practicing before the SEC or taking part in future public or private offerings.

Section 17 of the Securities Act[72] is similar to Rule 10b-5, but relates only to the "offer and sale" of securities rather than the "purchase and sale." There is no private right of action under Section 17 which means the SEC or criminal authorities can bring actions pursuant to Section 17, but private investors cannot.

Failure to properly register pursuant to Section 5 or to qualify for an exemption is a violation of Section 12(a)(1) of the Securities Act.[73] Unlike allegations of fraud pursuant to Rule 10b-5, no scienter is required to establish a violation of Section 12(a)(1). Violations of Section 12(a)(1) give investors a one-year right to rescind the purchase. Even in the absence of a violation of Section 12(a)(1) or other provision, issuers may offer to rescind purchases to disgruntled shareholders. This does not eliminate all liability, but reduces the potential damages that shareholders could allege for such violations.

---

[72] Securities Act of 1933, Pub. L. No. 73-22, § 17, 48 Stat. 74.
[73] *Id.* § 12(a)(1).

Section 20(a) of the Exchange Act[74] provides liability for "control persons," including any person who directly or indirectly controls any person liable pursuant to Section 10 or Rule 10b-5. This means that officers, directors, or controlling shareholders who cause the company to commit a violation of the securities laws, may be personally liable.

In addition, remember that any conviction or judgment for securities fraud or securities violations could prevent the convicted party from engaging in future offerings pursuant to the bad boy provisions discussed in Chapter 5.

Most state securities statutes also include anti-fraud provisions. Many states also have rescission statutes that say if a sponsor offers to rescind an investor's purchase and refund the purchase price plus interest, the investor cannot refuse such offer and then later bring suit against the issuer. So if XYZ realized that it had inadvertently violated state law in a private sale of common stock, it could make a rescission offer to all of the investors. Any investors who refuse the rescission would be prohibited from bringing an action under state law, but claims under federal law may remain

Often, the facts of investigations into alleged securities malfeasance support violations of both state and federal laws, so state and federal authorities may coordinate on their investigations. Typically, one agency will take the lead in the investigation. The lead investigator will depend on the size and scope of the investigation, the relative agency workload capacities and other factors.

Finally, in the event of especially bad behavior, state or federal criminal authorities can file criminal charges against the issuers and its principals. Historically, federal prosecutors only filed criminal charges in the most egregious financial crimes, but over the last twenty years, criminal charges and investigations relating to securities offerings and trading have become more common. In particular, the US Attorney's office in New York has been quite proactive in prosecuting criminal securities offenses. Again, there is frequently cooperation in these matters between the SEC, Department of Justice, Internal Revenue Service, Federal Bureau of Investigations, and state agencies in conducting these investigations.

---

[74] Securities Exchange Act of 1934, Pub. L. No. 73-291, § 20(a), 48 Stat. 881.

10

Practical Guidance on Regulation D Offerings

Transaction Agreements

At the outset of an offering, the issuer may put together a term sheet describing the contemplated terms of the offering to discuss with potential investors to see if there is any interest in the offering. The term sheet is typically not binding, but is used as a sales and negotiation tool.

Once the terms of the offering are determined, the terms and conditions of the purchase will be set forth in a Subscription Agreement. The Subscription Agreement is the document where the investor formally agrees to purchase the offered securities. The Subscription Agreement also typically includes investor representations about their residency, investment intent, and accredited status as well as receipt of the offering materials and any other information necessary for their investment decision. Exhibit C contains an example of a basic Rule 506 Subscription Agreement.

Sometimes, in more complex offerings, the terms may be set forth in a Securities Purchase Agreement (often called a "SPA") and/or an Investors Rights Agreement (the "IRA"). These documents are typically used for transactions where the security itself is more complex, like a convertible or preferred security, or transactions where the investor negotiated special rights and protections, such as management rights, registration rights, information, voting covenants, or designated board seats. If the security is preferred stock, there may also be a Designation of Rights describing the terms of the security itself.

The issuer will also need to provide prospective investors with its governance documents. Corporations typically have articles of incorporation and bylaws and may have a shareholders' agreement detailing transfer restrictions, management rights or other provisions. Limited liability companies typically have an operating agreement or limited liability company agreement that describes the attributes of its membership interests, as well as management rights, transfer restrictions, and other relevant matters. Similarly, the terms of limited partnership interests, management rights, transfer restrictions, and other matters related to the operation of limited partnerships are typically described in a limited partnership agreement or similar document.

Common and preferred stock for non-public corporations is typically evidenced by a stock certificate. Occasionally limited liability company or partnership interests are certificated, but more commonly limited liability company interests and limited partnership interests for private companies are not certificated. Certificated securities should include appropriate legends on the back such as the one set forth in Chapter 5. Non-certificated securities should include appropriate legends describing applicable transfer restrictions in the Subscription Agreement or Securities Purchase Agreement or, if applicable, shareholder agreement, limited partnership agreement, or operating agreement.

Next, the offering and issuance of securities should be properly authorized by the issuer's board of directors, manager, general partner, or other authorized management party. If amendments to the issuer's articles of incorporation are required to increase the number of authorized shares or a Certificate of Designation is needed to create a new class of stock, or if the issuer's governance documents otherwise require, approval of the shareholders may be required. Applicable state law and the issuer's internal governance documents will dictate exactly what needs to be included in this authorization, but Appendix E includes an example of a typical board resolution for a corporate issuer like XYZ, Inc.

If the issuer is conducting an offering pursuant to Rule 505 or Rule 506, it will also need a Bad Boy certificate certifying its compliance with the applicable disqualification provisions. Appendix D contains a typical Bad Boy certificate for Rule 506 offerings.

Reg D and the Internet

Historically, little to no information about legitimate private placement offerings was permitted on the Internet due to the restrictions on public solicitation and advertising. While there was some limited regulatory guidance suggesting that a password protected website for exclusively accredited investors could post offering materials related to accredited investor offerings, most practitioners cautioned issuers not to post any information about their offerings on the Internet to avoid regulatory scrutiny. Issuers could continue to operate their regular company websites, provided that no information about their offering was included. Any information about the offering that was inadvertently posted on a website, mentioned in an interview, distributed by mass e-mail, or otherwise widely distributed could potentially bust the Regulation D exemption.

Issuers conducting Rule 506(c) offerings are no longer prohibited from advertising or solicitation, so these issuers will be permitted to post information about their offerings on their websites or other social media.

As discussed earlier, Rule 506(c) represents a significant change for regulators who have historically viewed any online advertising with great concern. Offerings advertised over the Internet were frequently unregistered offerings conducted in violation of Section 5 or offerings related to "pump and dump" schemes where chat room posters make inaccurate or exaggerated positive statements about a stock to raise its stock price while they sell their own shares. Similarly, some scammers short a stock and then take to chat rooms with false negative statements to drive the stock price down. As a result, issuers planning to conduct Rule 506(c) offerings should be very cautious when including offering information on their website or social media. Information regarding Rule 506(c) offerings should be clear, concise, and accurate and should avoid superlatives about potential profits. Statements like "get rich quick," "double your money in six months," or "no way to lose" are likely to raise regulatory ire and may give investors grounds for future litigation if such statements prove not to be accurate. As discussed earlier, a more conservative approach would be to use only basic information about the offering in public disclosures and then provide qualified accredited investors with more detailed disclosures about the offering and the issuer.

Potential Regulatory Changes in the Future

Changes to the Definition of Accredited Investor

There have been numerous discussions about whether the definition of Accredited Investor should be updated. Following the Dodd-Frank Act,[75] the definition was revised to exclude the value of the investor's primary residence from the determination of assets for purposes of the accredited investor standard. The definition has not otherwise been revised recently. Some commentators feel that the income and net worth thresholds need to be increased since they have not been updated for several years. Other commentators believe the definition should incorporate an element of experience or knowledge either in addition to the income or net worth threshold or as an alternative. Conceptually, it makes sense that a knowledgeable investor with relevant education and experience may be better able to understand the risks of an investment than a wealthy investor with limited experience with private offerings. The difficulty with this concept is finding a reasonable and objective way to determine whether prospective investors have sufficient experience with investments that they require fewer protections than other investors.

Some commentators suggest adding a qualification for "assets invested" to ensure that only investors with substantial funds invested in the market qualify as accredited since those investors are likely to have more experience with investments. New investors would have to demonstrate investment history with registered securities (which are theoretically less risky) before they would be considered accredited.

The Commission has indicated that it will analyze this definition in the future and may propose changes. There is no way to predict what changes may be proposed or the timing for adoption of these changes, so issuers should check with their counsel to verify the correct definition of "Accredited Investor" at the commencement of their offering.

Additional Reg D 506 protections

Simultaneously with the adoption of the new regulations creating Rule 506(c), the Commission issued a new proposal for further revisions to

---

[75] Dodd–Frank Act, Pub. L. No. 111–203, 124 Stat. 1376-2223 (2010).

Regulation D. The proposal was designed to create additional investor protections to offset some of the concerns raised by the JOBs Act, especially with respect to Rule 506(c). The proposal, which has not yet been adopted as of the date of this publication, included several components related to Rule 506(c) offerings:

- Form D must be filed at least fifteen days prior to the commencement of a Rule 506(c) offering and a closing amendment must be filed within thirty days after the conclusion of the offering.
- Form D would be amended to include additional information such as the issuer's website address, identification of any parties who control the issuer other than the "related persons" currently required to be disclosed, more detail about the issuer's industry, the issuer's size, the issuer's trading symbol, additional detail about investors participating in the offering, additional detail about the use of proceeds, the types of general solicitation used, and the method of accreditation verification employed.
- Issuers would be disqualified from relying on Rule 506 for one year if, at any time in the prior five years, the issuer failed to comply with the Reg D filing requirements with respect to a Rule 506 offering.
- New Rule 509[76] that would require certain legends in Rule 506(c) solicitation materials.
- Rule 156[77] of the Securities Act governs the use of sales literature by investment companies. The SEC's proposal would extend the application of Rule 156 to sales literature used by private funds.
- All general solicitation materials used in Rule 506(c) offerings would need to be provided to the SEC no later than the date of first use of such materials.

The rule proposal has been controversial because it highlights the conflict between simplifying the offering process to make it easier and more efficient for issuers to conduct offerings and protecting the investing public, who may or may not be able to fend for themselves. Many commentators in the capital raising community are concerned that

---

[76] 17 C.F.R. § 230.509.
[77] *Id.* § 230.156.

these proposed revisions would place a significant and expensive burden on issuers, making it more difficult to conduct offerings. Further, in some cases, an issuer may begin an offering down one road and then change its plan as the offering proceeds. Prefiling requirements would make this type of change virtually impossible. Other commentators feel these provisions provide little burden on issuers and would provide investors additional disclosures necessary to their consideration of a potential offer. Further, many of the provisions would make it easier for the SEC to identify problematic offerings at the outset.

This rule proposal was issued in July 2013 and remains in flux. The Commission may abandon the proposal entirely, or it may adopt a revised version.

Seeking Counsel

Experienced securities counsel is critical for companies planning to engage in offerings of securities. The state and federal regulatory landscape for private offerings is complex and subject to frequent changes. When seeking appropriate legal counsel for a private offering, you should ensure that they have experience with Regulation D offerings, Section 4(a)(2), and blue sky state compliance, as well as experience with the preparation of governance documents, disclosure documents, subscription agreements and other offering documents, and the preparation and filing of Form D. Your local bar association may be able to direct you to attorneys with experience in this area.

Broker-Dealers and Finders

Brokers and dealers of securities are required to be registered under Section 15 of the Securities Exchange Act.[78] For SEC purposes, "broker" is defined as "any person engaged in the business of effecting transactions for the account of others" and dealer is defined as "any person engaged in the business of buying and selling securities for his own account, through a broker or otherwise." These definitions generally encompass anyone buying or selling someone else's securities. The

---

[78] Securities Exchange Act of 1934, Pub. L. No. 73-291, § 15, 48 Stat. 881.

issuer is generally not considered a broker under federal law when it is selling its own securities and is generally not considered a dealer provided they are not in the "business" of buying and selling their securities. Employees of the issuers are generally also exempt provided they are not routinely engaged in the business of effecting securities transactions, not associated with a broker-dealer, and they do not receive separate compensation for such sales.

Most states also have laws requiring the registration of brokers and dealers as well as similar exemptions for issuers and their employees; however, state laws vary. As discussed in Chapter 7, the New York registration scheme is different and may require issuer registration.

The exemptions that apply to officers, directors, and employees of the issuer selling issuer securities generally do not apply to third parties. Accordingly, if the issuer engages someone to help sell its securities, that person should generally be registered as a broker-dealer. Some people claim to be exempt from the broker-dealer requirements because they are "finders" and not brokers. There is no formal "finders" exemption from the broker-dealer requirements. SEC guidance on broker-dealer registration looks at a number of factors including: (i) whether the third party is involved in the solicitation, negotiation, or execution of the offering; (ii) whether the third party's compensation is tied to the outcome or size of the transaction, involves trailing commissions or involves other transaction-related compensation; (iii) whether the third party is generally involved in the business of effecting or facilitating transactions; and (iv) whether the third party handles securities or funds of others.

If the "finder" helps to solicit investors or negotiate the offering, is paid compensation related to the success of the offering, is engaged primarily in the business of selling securities or handles any of the offering funds, it may need to register.

Registration may not be necessary if a third party merely makes an introduction where no compensation is paid. Likewise, issuers may engage financial analysts to provide advice about the structure of the offering, provided that the analysts are not involved with the sale of securities.

Over the last few years, both the SEC and FINRA have taken a much closer look at "finders" to determine whether they are acting as unregistered brokers. In 2015, FINRA adopted new regulations clarifying that it is improper to pay compensation to any person who is not registered as a broker-dealer pursuant to Section 15(a) of the Exchange Act,[79] but who is required to be registered. Before engaging someone to assist with your offering, you should determine whether they are a licensed broker-dealer. You can verify a broker's registration status, qualifications and review any disclosure events at FINRA's BrokerCheck website: http://www.finra.org/Investors/ToolsCalculators/BrokerCheck/.

If the person is not registered, consider whether their services are truly in the nature of financial advice or whether they are actually assisting with selling securities. Also, consider whether their compensation is tied to the success of the offering. If so, you may want to engage someone else. Working with an unregistered broker-dealer could bring unwanted administrative agency scrutiny to your offering and someone who flouts their own registration requirements may not be diligent in adhering to the legal requirements for your private placement offering.

For example, if XYZ is conducting a Rule 506(b) offering and XYZ's accountant volunteers to introduce XYZ's President to his close friend Artie Angello, an angel investor, that introduction would not cause the accountant to be a broker. On the other hand, if the accountant offered to approach several of his contacts about the offering in exchange for 4 percent of the proceeds raised by his contacts, the accountant may need to be registered as a broker.

When in doubt, check with your counsel before engaging any third party to assist with your offering.

Other Considerations

Certain offering transactions may raise other regulatory issues. For example, an issuer that plans to make investments in other companies has two other potential legal considerations. First, the issuer may be required

---

[79] *Id.*

to register as an investment company under the Investment Company Act. Second, either the issuer or its principles may be required to register as investment advisers pursuant to the Investment Advisers Act.

The Investment Company Act[80] requires issuers engaged primarily in the business of investing or trading in securities to register with the SEC. There are two primary exemptions from the Investment Company Act that venture funds, hedge funds, and other private equity funds frequently rely upon. Section 3(c)(1) exempts investment companies with fewer than one hundred equity owners that do not propose to make a public offering. Section 3(c)(7) exempts investment companies that are exclusively owned by Qualified Purchasers. Qualified Purchasers are generally institutions with at least $25 million in investments or individuals with at least $5 million in investments.

The Investment Advisers Act[81] generally requires anyone who advises others about the value of securities or the advisability of purchasing or selling securities to register as an investment adviser. In the private offering context, this is typically a concern for issuers acting as funds investing in multiple other companies. The principals of the issuer may need to register as investment advisers either with applicable states or the SEC, depending on the total amount of assets under management. There are certain exemptions from the investment adviser registration requirements. The most commonly used exemption in this context is the private investment adviser exemption, which applies to advisers with fewer than fifteen clients during the preceding twelve months that do not generally hold themselves out to the public as investment advisers.

The application of the Investment Company Act and Investment Advisers Act rules and exemptions is complex, so you should confer with your counsel to determine if these laws impact your offering.

---

[80] The Investment Company Act, Pub. L. No. 76-768, 54 Stat. 789 (1940).
[81] Investment Advisers Act of 1940, 15 U.S.C. §§ 80b-1 to 80b-21.

11

Frequently Asked Questions

Q: **I need to raise money for my company. What do I need to do?**

A: One way to raise capital for a company is to sell securities to investors giving them an ownership stake in the company. The sale of any securities in the United States must either be registered with the Securities and Exchange Commission or exempt from registration under federal and state law. Regulation D is a commonly used federal exemption for private placement offerings. If the issuer complies with all of the rules and conditions for the appropriate Regulation D exemption and applicable state exemptions, the sale of securities will not need to be registered.

Q: **Do I need to do anything if I am just selling to a few people?**

A: Every sale of securities must be either registered with the Securities and Exchange Commission or exempt from registration. Some exemptions require notice filings or have other conditions, while others are "self-executing" and do not require any filings. Before starting an offering, you should consult with your attorney to determine the best exemption alternative for your transaction.

Q: **If I sell preferred securities, partnership interests or interests in an orange grove, do I need to comply with the securities laws?**

A: Registration requirements apply to the sale of any security, which encompasses far more than common stock. Preferred stock, limited liability company or partnership interests, convertible debt, notes, certain fractional undivided interests in oil, gas or mineral rights, options or other "investment contracts" can all be securities. The key case interpreting the scope of "investment contracts" held that an investment in an orange grove where the investor had no role in the actual operation of the grove was a security and was therefore subject to securities laws. Courts have also found investment contracts with charter boats, real estate and other investment opportunities. You should confirm with your counsel whether securities laws will apply to your contemplated transaction.

Q: Can I sell to friends and family even if they are not accredited investors?

A: You can sell securities to unaccredited investors pursuant to offerings conducted under Regulation D Rule 504, Rule 505 or Rule 506(b), however offerings to unaccredited investors may be subject to additional limitations. For example, offerings to unaccredited investors pursuant to Rule 505 or 506(b) are limited to thirty-five unaccredited investors and are subject to enhanced disclosure requirements. As a result, offerings that include even one unaccredited investor are typically more expensive and more burdensome than offerings to exclusively accredited investors. In addition, unaccredited investors in Rule 506(b) must be sophisticated enough to understand the risks of the offering or have an advisor that is sophisticated.

Q: I heard that crowdfunding is legal now, so I can just sell my securities over the Internet. Is that true?

A: No! The sale of securities pursuant to "crowdfunding" through the crowdfunding exemption created by the JOBs Act (as opposed to Regulation A, Regulation D or types of offerings), is subject to investor limitations, disclosure requirements and limitations on the manner of sale. More importantly, as of the date of this book, federal crowdfunding regulations have not yet been adopted, so federal crowdfunding is not yet permitted. Some states have adopted intrastate crowdfunding statutes that have gone into effect, so you should check with your counsel before any contemplated crowdfunding offering to confirm the current status of the applicable regulations. See Chapter 6 for more information on crowdfunding.

Q: I know a guy who promises that he can find investors for my company. Is that a problem?

A: Maybe. Generally, only registered broker-dealers are authorized to sell securities in exchange for compensation (which includes any type of remuneration). Just because someone calls themselves a "finder" does not necessary mean they are not subject to the broker-dealer registration requirements under state and federal law. See Chapter 10 for more detail on this issue.

Q: What government agencies will I need to deal with?

A: Securities offerings in the United States are subject to both federal law and the laws of any state where investors reside, and administered by the Securities and Exchange Commission and by state securities commissions. If any investors reside outside of the United States, the laws of the investor's residence may also apply.

Q: How can I market my securities?

A: Generally, advertising and public solicitation are prohibited for Regulation D private placement securities offerings. Prospective investors should be people with whom the issuer has a pre-existing relationship. This prohibition on advertising and solicitation would include offering securities through advertisements, websites, email blasts, conferences or other public venues. Public solicitation and advertising may be permitted for certain offerings pursuant to Regulation D Rule 504 and 506(c), provided certain other conditions are met.

Q: Do I need an attorney to help with my private placement?

A: Yes, you should engage an experienced securities attorney to assist with your offering. Securities laws are complex and change frequently and failure to comply with the securities laws can have devastating effects on the issuer and its principals. This book will give you some insight into the basics of Regulation D, but it is no substitute for legal counsel.

Q: What is the best Regulation D exemption?

A: Different exemptions may be appropriate for different offering structures, but accredited-only offerings pursuant to Regulation D Rule 506 are the most popular alternative because there is no dollar or investor limit (assuming all investors are accredited), mandatory disclosure obligations are limited and state regulatory requirements are minimal since Rule 506 securities are considered "covered securities."

APPENDICES

APPENDIX A

RESOURCES

- www.sec.gov: This is the US Securities and Exchange Commission website and it has information about proposed and finalized regulations, enforcement actions, SEC guidance on regulatory issues and electronic company filings in the EDGAR database. Check *Small Business and the SEC*, U.S. SECURITIES & EXCHANGE COMMISSION, http://www.sec.gov/info/smallbus/qasbsec.htm for a summary of federal regulations impacting small business.

- www.nasaa.org: This is the website for the North American Securities Administrators Association. NASAA is comprised primarily of state securities regulators.

- www.edfr.gov: This website contains all of the Code of Federal Regulations. Search for "Securities Act of 1933" to pull up Title 17, Part 230 with all of the Securities Act regulations, including Regulation D (§ 230.501-230.506).

APPENDIX B

FORM D

Form D must be filed electronically with the SEC as described in Chapter 8. The following is a paper version of the Form so you can see the information that would be required. You can also find this form on the SEC website at https://www.sec.gov/about/forms/formd.pdf.

FORM D
Notice of Exempt
ffering of Securities

U.S. Securities and Exchange Commission
Washington, DC 20549

(See instructions beginning on page 5)

Intentional misstatements or omissions of fact constitute federal criminal violations. See 18 U.S.C. 1001.

OMB APPROVAL
OMB Number: 3235-0076
Expires: September 30, 2016
Estimated average burden hours per response: 4.00

Item 1. Issuer's Identity

Name of Issuer

Previous Name(s)   ☐ None

Jurisdiction of Incorporation/Organization

Year of Incorporation/Organization
(Select one)
○ Over Five Years Ago   ○ Within Last Five Years (specify year)   ○ Yet to Be Formed

Entity Type (Select one)
☐ Corporation
☐ Limited Partnership
☐ Limited Liability Company
☐ General Partnership
☐ Business Trust
☐ Other (Specify)

(If more than one Issuer is filing this notice, check this box ☐ *and identify additional Issuer(s) by attaching Items 1 and 2 Continuation Page(s).)*

Item 2. Principal Place of Business and Contact Information

Street Address 1

Street Address 2

City   State/Province/Country   ZIP/Postal Code   Phone No.

Item 3. Related Persons

Last Name   First Name   Middle Name

Street Address 1   Street Address 2

City   State/Province/Country   ZIP/Postal Code

Relationship(s):   ☐ Executive Officer   ☐ Director   ☐ Promoter

Clarification of Response (if necessary)

(Identify additional related persons by checking this box ☐ *and attaching Item 3 Continuation Page(s).)*

Item 4. Industry Group   (Select one)

○ **Agriculture**
Banking and Financial Services
   ○ Commercial Banking
   ○ Insurance
   ○ Investing
   ○ Investment Banking
   ○ Pooled Investment Fund
   If selecting this industry group, also select one fund type below and answer the question below:
   ○ Hedge Fund
   ○ Private Equity Fund
   ○ Venture Capital Fund
   ○ Other Investment Fund
   Is the issuer registered as an investment company under the Investment Company Act of 1940? ○ Yes ○ No
○ Other Banking & Financial Services

○ **Business Services**
Energy
   ○ Electric Utilities
   ○ Energy Conservation
   ○ Coal Mining
   ○ Environmental Services
   ○ Oil & Gas
   ○ Other Energy
Health Care
   ○ Biotechnology
   ○ Health Insurance
   ○ Hospitals & Physicians
   ○ Pharmaceuticals
   ○ Other Health Care
○ **Manufacturing**
Real Estate
   ○ Commercial

○ Construction
○ REITS & Finance
○ Residential
○ Other Real Estate
○ **Retailing**
○ **Restaurants**
Technology
   ○ Computers
   ○ Telecommunications
   ○ Other Technology
Travel
   ○ Airlines & Airports
   ○ Lodging & Conventions
   ○ Tourism & Travel Services
   ○ Other Travel
○ **Other**

SEC1972 (9/13)   Form D 1

FORM D

U.S. Securities and Exchange Commission
Washington, DC 20549

Item 5. Issuer Size   (Select one)

Revenue Range (for issuer not specifying "hedge" or "other investment" fund in Item 4 above)

OR

- O No Revenues
- O $1 - $1,000,000
- O $1,000,001 - $5,000,000
- O $5,000,001 - $25,000,000
- O $25,000,001 - $100,000,000
- O Over $100,000,000
- O Decline to Disclose
- O Not Applicable

Aggregate Net Asset Value Range (for issuer specifying "hedge" or "other investment" fund in Item 4 above)

- O No Aggregate Net Asset Value
- O $1 - $5,000,000
- O $5,000,001 - $25,000,000
- O $25,000,001 - $50,000,000
- O $50,000,001 - $100,000,000
- O Over $100,000,000
- O Decline to Disclose
- O Not Applicable

Item 6. Federal Exemptions and Exclusions Claimed   (Select all that apply)

- ☐ Rule 504(b)(1) (not (i), (ii) or (iii))
- ☐ Rule 504(b)(1)(i)
- ☐ Rule 504(b)(1)(ii)
- ☐ Rule 504(b)(1)(iii)
- ☐ Rule 505
- ☐ Rule 506(b)
- ☐ Rule 506(c)
- ☐ Securities Act Section 4(a)(5)

Investment Company Act Section 3(c)

- ☐ Section 3(c)(1)
- ☐ Section 3(c)(2)
- ☐ Section 3(c)(3)
- ☐ Section 3(c)(4)
- ☐ Section 3(c)(5)
- ☐ Section 3(c)(6)
- ☐ Section 3(c)(7)

- ☐ Section 3(c)(9)
- ☐ Section 3(c)(10)
- ☐ Section 3(c)(11)
- ☐ Section 3(c)(12)
- ☐ Section 3(c)(13)
- ☐ Section 3(c)(14)

Item 7. Type of Filing

O New Notice   **OR**   O Amendment

Date of First Sale in this Offering: _____   **OR**   ☐ First Sale Yet to Occur

Item 8. Duration of Offering

Does the issuer intend this offering to last more than one year?   ☐ Yes   ☐ No

Item 9. Type(s) of Securities Offered   (Select all that apply)

- ☐ Equity
- ☐ Debt
- ☐ Option, Warrant or Other Right to Acquire Another Security
- ☐ Security to be Acquired Upon Exercise of Option, Warrant or Other Right to Acquire Security

- ☐ Pooled Investment Fund Interests
- ☐ Tenant-in-Common Securities
- ☐ Mineral Property Securities
- ☐ Other (describe)

Item 10. Business Combination Transaction

Is this offering being made in connection with a business combination transaction, such as a merger, acquisition or exchange offer?   ☐ Yes   ☐ No

Clarification of Response (if necessary)

FORM D   U.S. Securities and Exchange Commission
                              Washington, DC 20549

Item 11. Minimum Investment

Minimum investment accepted from any outside investor $ [   ]

Item 12. Sales Compensation

Recipient   Recipient CRD Number

[   ]   [   ] ☐ No CRD Number

(Associated) Broker or Dealer   ☐ None   (Associated) Broker or Dealer CRD Number

[   ]   [   ] ☐ No CRD Number

Street Address 1   Street Address 2

[   ]   [   ]

City   State/Province/Country   ZIP/Postal Code

[   ]   [   ]   [   ]

States of Solicitation   ☐ All States

☐ AL	☐ AK	☐ AZ	☐ AR	☐ CA	☐ CO	☐ CT	☐ DE	☐ DC	☐ FL	☐ GA	☐ HI	☐ ID
☐ IL	☐ IN	☐ IA	☐ KS	☐ KY	☐ LA	☐ ME	☐ MD	☐ MA	☐ MI	☐ MN	☐ MS	☐ MO
☐ MT	☐ NE	☐ NV	☐ NH	☐ NJ	☐ NM	☐ NY	☐ NC	☐ ND	☐ OH	☐ OK	☐ OR	☐ PA
☐ RI	☐ SC	☐ SD	☐ TN	☐ TX	☐ UT	☐ VT	☐ VA	☐ WA	☐ WV	☐ WI	☐ WY	☐ PR

(Identify additional person(s) being paid compensation by checking this box ☐ and attaching Item 12 Continuation Page(s).)

Item 13. Offering and Sales Amounts

(a) Total Offering Amount $ [   ]   **OR** ☐ Indefinite

(b) Total Amount Sold $ [   ]

(c) Total Remaining to be Sold $ [   ]   **OR** ☐ Indefinite
   (Subtract (a) from (b))

Clarification of Response (if necessary)

[   ]

Item 14. Investors

Check this box ☐ if securities in the offering have been or may be sold to persons who do not qualify as accredited investors, and enter the number of such non-accredited investors who already have invested in the offering: [   ]

Enter the total number of investors who already have invested in the offering: [   ]

Item 15. Sales Commissions and Finders' Fees Expenses

Provide separately the amounts of sales commissions and finders' fees expenses, if any. If an amount is not known, provide an estimate and check the box next to the amount.

                              Sales Commissions $ [   ]   ☐ Estimate

Clarification of Response (if necessary)   Finders' Fees $ [   ]   ☐ Estimate

[   ]

FORM D

U.S. Securities and Exchange Commission

Washington, DC 20549

Item 16. Use of Proceeds

Provide the amount of the gross proceeds of the offering that has been or is proposed to be used for payments to any of the persons required to be named as executive officers, directors or promoters in response to Item 3 above. If the amount is unknown, provide an estimate and check the box next to the amount.

$ [   ]   ☐ Estimate

Clarification of Response (if necessary)

Signature and Submission

Please verify the information you have entered and review the Terms of Submission below before signing and submitting this notice.

Terms of Submission. In Submitting this notice, each identified issuer is:

Notifying the SEC and/or each State in which this notice is filed of the offering of securities described and undertaking to furnish them, upon written request, in accordance with applicable law, the information furnished to offerees.[*]

Irrevocably appointing each of the Secretary of the SEC and the Securities Administrator or other legally designated officer of the State in which the issuer maintains its principal place of business and any State in which this notice is filed, as its agents for service of process, and agreeing that these persons may accept service on its behalf, of any notice, process or pleading, and further agreeing that such service may be made by registered or certified mail, in any Federal or state action, administrative proceeding, or arbitration brought against the issuer in any place subject to the jurisdiction of the United States, if the action, proceeding or arbitration (a) arises out of any activity in connection with the offering of securities that is the subject of this notice, and (b) is founded, directly or indirectly, upon the provisions of: (i) the Securities Act of 1933, the Securities Exchange Act of 1934, the Trust Indenture Act of 1939, the Investment Company Act of 1940, or the Investment Advisers Act of 1940, or any rule or regulation under any of these statutes; or (ii) the laws of the State in which the issuer maintains its principal place of business or any State in which this notice is filed.

Certifying that, if the issuer is claiming a Regulation D exemption for the offering, the issuer is not disqualified from relying on Regulation D for one of the reasons stated in Rule 505(b)(2)(iii) or Rule 506(d).

[*] This undertaking does not affect any limits Section 102(a) of the National Securities Markets Improvement Act of 1996 ("NSMIA") [Pub. L. No. 104-290, 110 Stat. 3416 (Oct. 11, 1996)] imposes on the ability of States to require information. As a result, if the securities that are the subject of this Form D are "covered securities" for purposes of NSMIA, whether in all instances or due to the nature of the offering that is the subject of this Form D, States cannot routinely require offering materials under this undertaking or otherwise and can require offering materials only to the extent NSMIA permits them to do so under NSMIA's preservation of their anti-fraud authority.

Each identified issuer has read this notice, knows the contents to be true, and has duly caused this notice to be signed on its behalf by the undersigned duly authorized person. (Check this box ☐ and attach Signature Continuation Pages for signatures of issuers identified in Item 1 above but not represented by signer below.)

Issuer(s)

Name of Signer

Signature

Title

Date

Number of continuation pages attached: [   ]

Persons who respond to the collection of information contained in this form are not required to respond unless the form displays a currently valid OMB number.

FORM D

U.S. Securities and Exchange Commission
Washington, DC 20549

Instructions for Submitting a Form D Notice

General Instructions

Who must file: Each issuer of securities that sells its securities in reliance on an exemption provided in Regulation D or Section 4(a)(5) of the Securities Act of 1933 must file this notice containing the information requested with the U.S. Securities and Exchange Commission (SEC) and with the state(s) requiring it. If more than one issuer has sold its securitie in the same transaction, all issuers should be identified in one filing with the SEC, but some states may require a separate filing for each issuer or security sold.

When to file:

o An issuer must file a new notice with the SEC for each new offering of securities no later than 15 calendar days after the "date of first sale" of securities in the offering as explained in the Instruction to Item 7. For this purpose, the date of first sale is the date on which the first investor is irrevocably contractually committed to invest, which, depending on the terms and conditions of the contract, could be the date on which the issuer receives the investor's subscription agreement or check. An issuer may file the notice at any time before that if it has determined to make the offering. An issuer must file a new notice with each state that requires it at the time set by the state. For state filing information, go to www.NASAA.org. A mandatory capital commitment call does not constitute a new offering, but is made under the original offering, so no new Form D filing is required.

o An issuer may file an amendment to a previously filed notice at any time.

o An issuer must file an amendment to a previously filed notice for an offering:

- to correct a material mistake of fact or error in the previously filed notice, as soon as practicable after discovery of the mistake or error;

- to reflect a change in the information provided in the previously filed notice, except as provided below, as soon as practicable after the change; and

- annually, on or before the first anniversary of the most recent previously filed notice, if the offering is continuing at that time.

When amendment is not required: An issuer is not required to file an amendment to a previously filed notice to reflect a change that occurs after the offering terminates or a change that occurs solely in the following information:

- the address or relationship to the issuer of a related person identified in response to Item 3;

- an issuer's revenues or aggregate net asset value;

- the minimum investment amount, if the change is an increase, or if the change, together with all other changes in that amount since the previously filed notice, does not result in a decrease of more than 10%;

- any address or state(s) of solicitation shown in response to Item 12;

- the total offering amount, if the change is a decrease, or if the change, together with all other changes in that amount since the previously filed notice, does not result in an increase of more than 10%;

- the amount of securities sold in the offering or the amount remaining to be sold;

- the number of non-accredited investors who have invested in the offering, as long as the change does not increase the number to more than 35;

- the total number of investors who have invested in the offering; and

- the amount of sales commissions, finders' fees or use of proceeds for payments to executive officers, directors or promoters, if the change is a decrease, or if the change, together with all other changes in that amount since the previously filed notice, does not result in an increase of more than 10%.

Saturdays, Sundays and holidays: If the date on which a notice or an amendment to a previously filed notice is required to be filed falls on a Saturday, Sunday or holiday, the due date is the first business day following.

Amendment content: An issuer that files an amendment to a previously filed notice must provide current information in response to all items of this Form D, regardless of why the amendment is filed.

How to file: Issuers must file this notice with the SEC in electronic format. For state filing information, go to www.NASAA.org.

Filing fee: There is no federal filing fee. For information on state filing fees, go to www. NASAA.org.

Definitions of terms: Terms used but not defined in this form that are defined in Rule 405 and Rule 501 under the Securities Act of 1933, 17 CFR 230.405 and 230.501, have the meanings given to them in those rules.

FORM D

Item-by-Item Instructions

Item 1. Issuer's Identity. Identify each legal entity issuing any securities being reported as being offered by entering its full name; any previous name used within the past five years; and its jurisdiction of incorporation or organization, type of legal entity, and year of incorporation or organization within the past five years or status as formed over five years ago or not yet formed. If more than one entity is issuing the securities, identify a primary issuer in the first fields shown on the first page of the form, checking the box provided, and identify additional issuers by attaching Items 1 and 2 continuation page(s).

Item 2. Principal Place of Business and Contact Information. Enter a full street address of the issuer's principal place of business. Post office box numbers and "In care of" addresses are not acceptable. Enter a contact telephone number for the issuer. If you identified more than one issuer in response to Item 1, enter the requested information for the primary issuer you identified in response to that item and, at your option, for any or all of the other issuers you identified on your Item 1 and 2 continuation page(s).

Item 3. Related Persons. Enter the full name and address of each person having the specified relationships with any issuer and identify each relationship:

    • Each executive officer and director of the issuer and person performing similar functions (title alone is not determinative) for the issuer, such as the general and managing partners of partnerships and managing members of limited liability companies; and

    • Each person who has functioned directly or indirectly as a promoter of the issuer within the past five years of the later of the first sale of securities or the date upon which the Form D filing was required to be made.

If necessary to prevent the information supplied from being misleading, also provide a clarification in the space provided.

Identify additional persons having the specified relationships by checking the box provided and attaching Item 3 continuation page(s).

Item 4. Industry Group. Select the issuer's industry group. If the issuer or issuers can be categorized in more than one industry group, select the industry group that most accurately reflects the use of the bulk of the proceeds of the offering. For purposes of this filing, use the ordinary dictionary and commonly understood meanings of the terms identifying the industry group.

Item 5. Issuer Size.

    • **Revenue Range** (for issuers that do not specify "Hedge Fund" or "Other Investment Fund" in response to Item 4): Enter the revenue range of the issuer or of all the issuers together for the most recently completed fiscal year available, or, if not in existence for a fiscal year, revenue range to date. Domestic SEC reporting companies should state revenues in accordance with Regulation S-X under the Securities Exchange Act of 1934. Domestic non-reporting companies should state revenues in accordance with U.S. Generally Accepted Accounting Principles (GAAP). Foreign issuers should calculate revenues in U.S. dollars and state them in accordance with U.S. GAAP, home country GAAP or International Financial Reporting Standards. If the issuer(s) declines to disclose its revenue range, enter "Decline to Disclose." If the issuer's(s') business is intended to produce revenue but did not, enter "No Revenues." If the business is not intended to produce revenue (for example, the business seeks asset appreciation only), enter "Not Applicable."

    • **Aggregate Net Asset Value** (for issuers that specify "Hedge Fund" or "Other Investment Fund" in response to Item 4): Enter the aggregate net asset value range of the issuer or of all the issuers together as of the most recent practicable date. If the issuer(s) declines to disclose its aggregate net asset value range, enter "Decline to Disclose."

Item 6. Federal Exemption(s) and Exclusion(s) Claimed. Select the provision(s) being claimed to exempt the offering and resulting sales from the federal registration requirements under the Securities Act of 1933 and, if applicable, to exclude the issuer from the definition of "investment company" under the Investment Company Act of 1940. Select "Rule 504(b)(1) (not (i), (ii) or (iii))" only if the issuer is relying on the exemption in the introductory sentence of Rule 504 for offers and sales that satisfy all the terms and conditions of Rules 501 and 502(a), (c) and (d).

Item 7. Type of Filing. Indicate whether the issuer is filing a new notice or an amendment to a notice that was filed previously. If this is a new notice, enter the date of the first sale of securities in the offering or indicate that the first sale has "Yet to Occur." For this purpose, the date of first sale is the date on which the first investor is irrevocably contractually committed to invest, which, depending on the terms and conditions of the contract, could be the date on which the issuer receives the investor's subscription agreement or check.

Item 8. Duration of Offering. Indicate whether the issuer intends the offering to last for more than one year.

FORM D

Item-by-Item Instructions (Continued)

Item 9. Type(s) of Securities Offered. Select the appropriate type or types of securities offered as to which this notice is filed. If the securities are debt convertible into other securities, however, select "Debt" and any other appropriate types of securities except for "Equity." For purposes of this filing, use the ordinary dictionary and commonly understood meanings of these categories. For instance, equity securities would be securities that represent proportional ownership in an issuer, such as ordinary common and preferred stock of corporations and partnership and limited liability company interests; debt securities would be securities representing money loaned to an issuer that must be repaid to the investor at a later date; pooled investment fund interests would be securities that represent ownership interests in a pooled or collective investment vehicle; tenant-in-common securities would be securities that include an undivided fractional interest in real property other than a mineral property; and mineral property securities would be securities that include an undivided interest in an oil, gas or other mineral property.

Item 10. Business Combination Transaction. Indicate whether or not the offering is being made in connection with a business combination, such as an exchange (tender) offer or a merger, acquisition, or other transaction of the type described in paragraph (a)(1), (2) or (3) of Rule 145 under the Securities Act of 1933. Do not include an exchange (tender) offer for a class of the issuer's own securities. If necessary to prevent the information supplied from being misleading, also provide a clarification in the space provided.

Item 11. Minimum Investment. Enter the minimum dollar amount of investment that will be accepted from any outside investor. If the offering provides a minimum investment amount for outside investors that can be waived, provide the lowest amount below which a waiver will not be granted. If there is no minimum investment amount, enter "0." Investors will be considered outside investors if they are not employees, officers, directors, general partners, trustees (where the issuer is a business trust), consultants, advisors or vendors of the issuer, its parents, its majority owned subsidiaries, or majority owned subsidiaries of the issuer's parent.

Item 12. Sales Compensation. Enter the requested information for each person that has been or will be paid directly or indirectly any commission or other similar compensation in cash or other consideration in connection with sales of securities in the offering, including finders. Enter the CRD number for every person identified and any broker and dealer listed that has a CRD number. CRD numbers can be found at http://brokercheck.finra.org. A person that does not have a CRD number need not obtain one in order to be listed, and must be listed when required regardless of whether the person has a CRD number. In addition, check the State(s) in which the named person has solicited or intends to solicit investors. If more than five persons to be listed are associated persons of the same broker or dealer, enter only the name of the broker or dealer, its CRD number and street address, and the State(s) in which the named person has solicited or intends to solicit investors.

Item 13. Offering and Sales Amounts. Enter the dollar amount of securities being offered under a claim of federal exemption identified in Item 6 above. Also enter the dollar amount of securities sold in the offering as of the filing date. Select the "Indefinite" box if the amount being offered is undetermined or cannot be calculated at the present time, such as if the offering includes securities to be acquired upon the exercise or exchange of other securities or property and the exercise price or exchange value is not currently known or knowable. If an amount is definite but difficult to calculate without unreasonable effort or expense, provide a good faith estimate. The total offering and sold amounts should include all cash and other consideration to be received for the securities, including cash to be paid in the future under mandatory capital commitments. In offerings for consideration other than cash, the amounts entered should be based on the issuer's good faith valuation of the consideration. If necessary to prevent the information supplied from being misleading, also provide a clarification in the space provided.

Item 14. Investors. Indicate whether securities in the offering have been or may be sold to persons who do not qualify as accredited investors as defined in Rule 501(a), 17 CFR 230.501(a), and provide the number of such investors who have already invested in the offering. In addition, regardless of whether securities in the offering have been or may be sold to persons who do not qualify as accredited investors, specify the total number of investors who already have invested.

Item 15. Sales Commission and Finders' Fees Expenses. The information on sales commissions and finders' fees expenses may be given as subject to future contingencies.

Item 16. Use of Proceeds. No additional instructions.

Signature and Submission. An individual who is a duly authorized representative of each issuer identified must sign, date and submit this notice for the issuer. The capacity in which the individual is signing should be set forth in the "Title" field underneath the individual's name.

The name of the issuer(s) on whose behalf the notice is being submitted should be set forth in the "Issuer" field beside the individual's name; if the individual is signing on behalf of all issuers submitting the notice, the word "All" may be set forth in the "Issuer" field. Attach signature continuation page(s) to have different individuals sign on behalf of different issuer(s). Enter the number of continuation pages attached and included in the filing. If no continuation pages are attached, enter "0".

APPENDIX C

FORM OF SUBSCRIPTION AGREEMENT

The following is an example of a typical Regulation D Rule 506 accredited offering subscription agreement for corporate common stock. Remember that if you are conducting a Rule 506(c) offering, you will need to review additional documentation to establish accreditation of your investors. The form should be modified for other types of securities or entities and other situations, so be sure to check with your counsel about an appropriate Subscription Agreement for your company.

ABC INC.
A Delaware corporation

Subscription Documents

June 1, 2015

Investor Name: _____

THE SHARES OF STOCK OF ABC INC. REFERRED TO IN THESE SUBSCRIPTION DOCUMENTS HAVE NOT AND WILL NOT BE REGISTERED UNDER THE SECURITIES ACT OF 1933 (THE "SECURITIES ACT") OR ANY APPLICABLE STATE SECURITIES LAWS ("STATE ACTS") AND ARE RESTRICTED SECURITIES AS THAT TERM IS DEFINED IN RULE 144 UNDER THE SECURITIES ACT. THE SECURITIES MAY NOT BE OFFERED FOR SALE, SOLD, OR OTHERWISE TRANSFERRED EXCEPT PURSUANT TO AN EFFECTIVE REGISTRATION STATEMENT OR QUALIFICATION UNDER THE SECURITIES ACT AND APPLICABLE STATE ACTS OR PURSUANT TO AN EXEMPTION FROM REGISTRATION UNDER THE SECURITIES ACT AND APPLICABLE STATE ACTS, THE AVAILABILITY OF WHICH IS TO BE ESTABLISHED TO THE SATISFACTION OF ABC INC.

ABC INC. INVESTMENT PROCEDURES

Prospective investors must complete the following steps prior to the intended date of subscription:

1. Complete the attached Subscription Agreement including all information required on page SA-1, the investor information on pages SA-1 to SA-5 and sign on page SA-15.
2. Sign the two Signature Pages to the Shareholder Agreement attached as Exhibit A.
3. Return the entire completed original Subscription Agreement along with the Signature Pages to the Shareholder Agreement, at the address below, preferably no later than July 7, 2015 so that the Company may determine whether the prospective investor is eligible to subscribe for shares of common stock in the Company (the "Shares").
4. Send the Subscription Agreement and Shareholder Agreement Signature Pages and direct all questions regarding the completion of these documents to:

   ABC INC.
   Attn.: Fred Jones, CEO
   123 Elm Street
   Denver, Colorado 12345
   Fredj@abc.com
   (303) 123-4567

5. The Company will notify the prospective investor whether it is eligible to subscribe for Shares, and will provide notification of the next available subscription date (the "Offering Date"). We anticipate that the initial Offering Date will be July 10, 2015.
6. Please wire the intended subscription amount (the "Subscription Amount") to the Company prior to the Offering Date using the attached Payment Information Sheet. If the subscription is not accepted for any reason, the Subscription Amount will be returned to the prospective investor without interest.

7. Upon acceptance of the subscription, a copy of the executed Subscription Agreement signed as accepted on behalf of the Company, will be returned to the investor.

If requested by the Company, each prospective entity investor must provide evidence that the charter documents of the prospective investor permit it to make investments in securities such as the Shares, that all appropriate action has been taken by the prospective investor to authorize the investment and that the person(s) executing the Subscription Agreement has the authority to do so.

The Subscription Agreement, as well as payment in good funds of the Subscription Amount, must be received prior to the Offering Date, subject to the discretion of the Company to waive the "prior receipt" requirement.

If the prospective investor does not wish to subscribe for Shares, please return all of the enclosed documents to the above address. The enclosed documents may not be reproduced, duplicated or delivered to any other person.

ABC INC.
PAYMENT INFORMATION SHEET

Your bank should wire transfer only US Dollars via Fedwire to:

Bank: XYZ Bank
Address: 10987 Maplewood Drive, Lakewood, CO 80789
ABA: 987654321

For the Account of ABC INC., Account # 567891011

Please also have your bank send the following message (facsimile number (303) 123-4567) to Fred Jones, ABC INC:

"ABC INC. - We have credited your account at XYZ Bank, NA for $___ *(insert amount)* by order of _____ *(insert name of subscriber)* on _____ *(insert date)*. The Fedwire number of the wire transfer was _____ "

IMPORTANT

1) **Please have your bank identify on the wire transfer the name of the intended subscriber.**
2) **We recommend that your bank charge its wiring fees separately so that an even amount may be invested.**

ABC INC.
SUBSCRIPTION AGREEMENT

Amount of Subscription: $_____

Number of Shares:_____

ABC INC.

_____

_____

Attn: Fred Jones, Chief Executive Officer

Re: ABC INC. (the "Company")
Issuance of Shares of Common Stock ("Shares")

_____	Type of Investor - Please check one:
Name of Investor	
(Please Print or Type)	
Tax I.D. Number:_____	____ Individual
_____	____ Company
Name of person exercising	____ Corporation
investment discretion for	____ Limited Liability
subscriber	Company
(trustee or fiduciary, etc.)	____ Trust
	____ Tenants in Common
	____ Joint Tenants
	____ Other - Specify:
	_____

Residence or Principal Place of	Mailing address, if different:
Business Address:	
_____	_____
Name	Name
_____	_____
Street	Street
_____	_____
City, State, Zip Code	City, State, Zip Code

Attn:_____   Attn: _____

Telephone number: Telephone number:
( )_____   ( )_____
Facsimile number: Facsimile number:
( )_____   ( )_____
E-Mail: E-Mail:

_____   _____

Please send confirmation of a subscription for Shares, a copy of this Subscription Agreement and any other communications (including financial reports and distribution checks) to:

_____ residence or principal business address above
_____ mailing address above.

Ladies and Gentlemen:

The offer and sale of shares of common stock (the "Shares") in ABC INC., a Delaware corporation (the "Company"), to each investor (the "Investor") is not being registered under the Securities Act of 1933, as amended (the "Securities Act"), but rather is being made privately by the Company pursuant to the private placement exemption from registration provided in Section 4(a)(2) of the Securities Act and Rule 506 of Regulation D ("Regulation D") promulgated thereunder by the Securities and Exchange Commission (the "SEC").

The information requested in this Subscription Agreement is needed in order to ensure compliance with the appropriate regulations and to determine whether the Investor is an "accredited investor" as defined in Regulation D.

The Investor also understands and agrees that, although the Company will use its reasonable efforts to keep the information provided in the answers to this Subscription Agreement strictly confidential, the Company may present this Subscription Agreement and the information provided herein as it deems advisable if called upon to establish the availability under any applicable law of an exemption from registration of the Shares or if the contents are relevant to any issue in any action, suit, or proceeding to which the Company is a party.

By executing this Subscription Agreement, the Investor hereby agrees as follows:

I. SUBSCRIPTION FOR SHARES

The Investor agrees to become a shareholder of the Company (a "Shareholder") pursuant to the terms set forth in the shareholder agreement attached hereto as Exhibit A (the "Shareholder Agreement") and agrees to subscribes for and purchase shares of common stock of the Company (the "Shares") and to make a capital contribution ("Capital Contribution") to the Company on the terms provided for herein. The purchase price of the Shares is $_____ per share and the minimum investment amount is $_____. There are currently _____ Shares outstanding and after this offering, if fully subscribed, there will be _____ Shares outstanding. The Investor agrees to, and understands, the terms and conditions upon which the Shares are being offered and understands that the Company is in the development stage with no history of operations and may never achieve successful operations.

The Investor understands and agrees that the Company reserves the right to reject this subscription for any reason or no reason, in whole or in part and at any time prior to acceptance thereof. In the event of rejection of this subscription, any funds tendered to the Company, without interest, will be promptly returned to the Investor without deduction, along with this Subscription Agreement, and this Subscription Agreement shall have no force or effect. Upon acceptance of this subscription and the purchase price by the Company, the Investor shall be a Shareholder of the Company. The Investor hereby agrees that by its execution of this Subscription Agreement and upon acceptance hereof by the Company, it shall become a party to the Shareholder Agreement. The Investor shall sign and date the Signature Pages to the Shareholder Agreement attached hereto and promptly return them to the Company.

II. PAYMENT BY THE INVESTOR

The Investor will pay for the Shares concurrently with the submission of this Subscription Agreement to the Company (See attached Payment Information Sheet). Payment in good funds must be received prior to the Offering Date, subject to the discretion of the Company to waive such "prior receipt" requirement.

III. ELIGIBILITY REPRESENTATIONS OF THE INVESTOR

The Investor represents and warrants that:

General:

(Initial one and complete blanks)

_____   (1)   if the Investor is a corporation, partnership, trust or other
(Initial)   legal entity it is:
                 organized under the laws of: _____
                 and has its principal place
                 of business in: _____

          OR

_____   (2)   if the Investor is an individual, or beneficial ownership of
(Initial)   the Investor is held by an individual, such individual is of
                 legal age and is a resident of: _____

The individual(s) making the investment decision on behalf of the Investor is:

_____

Please provide the following information regarding such person:

Employment Information:

Name and address of employer: _____

Telephone number of employer: (   ) _____

Describe the person's occupation and any other business connections reflecting knowledge of and experience in financial and investment matters (service on boards of directors, professional licenses, etc.):

_____

_____

_____

Does such person have sufficient knowledge and experience in financial and business matters to be capable of evaluating the merits and risks associated with investing in the Company?

Yes _____   No _____

Accredited Investor Status:

Initial the appropriate spaces on the following pages indicating each applicable basis upon which the Investor qualifies as an accredited investor under Regulation D.

For Individual Investors Only

_____
(Initial)

(1) I certify that I am an accredited investor because I have an individual net worth, or my spouse and I have a combined net worth, in excess of $1,000,000, excluding the value of my primary residence.[82]

_____
(Initial)

(2) I certify that I am an accredited investor because I had individual income (exclusive of any income attributable to my spouse) of more than $200,000 for the past two years

---

[82] Indebtedness that is secured by the person's primary residence, up to the estimated fair market value of the primary residence at the time of the sale of securities, shall not be included as a liability (except that if the amount of such indebtedness outstanding at the time of sale of securities exceeds the amount outstanding 60 days before such time, other than as a result of the acquisition of the primary residence, the amount of such excess shall be included as a liability); and indebtedness that is secured by the person's primary residence in excess of the estimated fair market value of the primary residence at the time of the sale of securities shall be included as a liability.

or joint income with my spouse in excess of $300,000 in each of those years and I reasonably expect to reach the same income level in the current year.[83]

For Corporations, Limited Liability Companies or other Entities

(3) The Investor hereby certifies that it is an accredited investor because it has total assets in excess of $5,000,000 and was not formed for the specific purpose of acquiring the securities offered.

(Initial)

(4) The Investor hereby certifies that it is an accredited investor because all of its equity owners are accredited investors. *The Company may request information regarding the basis on which such equity owners are accredited.*

(Initial)

For Trusts

(5) The Investor hereby certifies that it is an accredited investor because it has total assets in excess of $5,000,000, was not formed for the specific purpose of acquiring the securities offered and its purchase is directed by a sophisticated person. *As used in the foregoing sentence, a "sophisticated person" is one who has such knowledge and experience in financial and business matters that it is capable of evaluating the merits and risks of the prospective investment.*

(Initial)

(6) The Investor hereby certifies that it is an accredited investor because it is (i) a bank as defined in Section 3(a)(2) of the Securities Act or a savings and loan association or other

(Initial)

---

[83] For purposes of this Subscription Agreement, individual income means adjusted gross income, as reported for federal income tax purposes, less any income attributable to a spouse or to property owned by a spouse, increased by the following amounts (but not including any amounts attributable to a spouse or to property owned by a spouse): (i) the amount of any tax-exempt interest income under Section 103 of the Internal Revenue Code of 1986, as amended (the "Code"), received, (ii) the amount of losses claimed as a limited partner in a limited partnership as reported on Schedule E of Form 1040, (iii) any deduction claimed for depletion under Section 611 *et seq.* of the Code, (iv) amounts contributed to an Individual Retirement Account (as defined in the Code) or Keogh retirement plan, (v) alimony paid and (vi) any elective contributions to a cash or deferred arrangement under Section 401(k) of the Code.

institution as defined in Section 3(a)(5)(A) of the Securities Act, (ii) acting in a fiduciary capacity, and (iii) subscribing for the purchase of the securities being offered on behalf of a trust account or accounts.

(7) The Investor hereby certifies that it is an accredited investor because it is a revocable trust which may be amended or revoked at any time by the grantors thereof and all of the grantors are accredited investors. *The Company may request information regarding the basis on which such equity owners are accredited.*

(Initial)

(8) The Investor hereby certifies that it is an accredited investor because (i)it was not formed for the specific purpose of investing in the Company; and (ii)the trustee or other authorized person making decisions with respect to the trust, and each settlor or other person who has contributed assets to the trust, is a person described in items (1), (2) or (3) of this Item.

(Initial)

For Banks, Savings and Loans and Similar Institutions

(9) The Investor hereby certifies that it is an accredited investor because it is a bank as defined in Section 3(a)(2) of the Securities Act or a savings and loan association or other institution as defined in Section 3(a)(5)(A) of the Securities Act acting in its individual capacity.

(Initial)

For Insurance Companies

(10) The Investor hereby certifies that it is an insurance company as defined in Section 2(13) of the Securities Act.

(Initial)

IV. REPRESENTATIONS AND COVENANTS OF THE INVESTOR

The Investor hereby represents and warrants to, and agrees with, the Company as follows:

A. <u>**Power and Authority.**</u> The Investor is authorized to enter into this Agreement, the Shareholder Agreement, and such other agreements, certificates, or other instruments as are required by or on behalf of the Investor in connection with its obligations under the Shareholder Agreement or in connection with this Agreement (collectively, the "Subscription Documents"). The Investor is authorized to perform its respective obligations under each Subscription Document, and to consummate the transactions that are the respective subjects of each Subscription Document. The signature of the respective individual signing any Subscription Document as, or on behalf of, the Investor is binding upon the Investor. The Investor is authorized and qualified to become a Shareholder in and authorized to make its Capital Contributions to, the Company and the person signing the Subscription Documents on behalf of the Investor has been duly authorized to do so.

B. <u>**Compliance with Laws and Other Instruments.**</u> The execution and delivery of the Subscription Documents by or on behalf of the Investor and the consummation of the transactions respectively contemplated by the Subscription Documents do not and will not conflict with or result in any violation of or default under any provision of any charter, bylaws, trust agreement, shareholder agreement, certificate, or other instrument to which the Investor is a party or by which the Investor or any of its properties is bound, or any permit, franchise, organizational document, agreement, indenture, order, judgment, decree, ordinance, statute, rule, regulation, or other law applicable to the Investor or the business or properties of the Investor.

C. <u>**Investor's Investment Intent.**</u> The Investor is acquiring the Shares for its own account for investment and not on behalf of any other person or entity. The Shares are being acquired for investment purposes and not with a view to any distribution, resale, subdivision, or fractionalization thereof in violation of the Securities Act or any other applicable domestic or foreign securities law, and the Investor has no present plans to enter into any contract, undertaking, agreement, or arrangement for any such distribution, resale, subdivision, or fractionalization.

D. **Availability of Information.** The Investor has carefully reviewed and is familiar with the terms of each Subscription Document and has reviewed all information provided in connection with this investment, including the Offering Memorandum attached hereto as Exhibit B. The Investor understands that the information provided is confidential and non-public and agrees that all such information shall be kept in confidence by the Investor and neither used by the Investor for the Investor's personal benefit (other than in connection with this Agreement) nor disclosed to any third party for any reason. The Company has made available to the Investor or its representatives all agreements, documents, records, and books that the Investor or its representatives have requested relating to an investment in the Company. The Investor has had a full opportunity to ask questions of and receive answers from the Company or a person acting on behalf of the Company concerning the terms and conditions of this investment, and all questions asked by the Investor have been adequately answered to the full satisfaction of the Investor. The Investor has obtained, in its judgment, sufficient information from the Company to evaluate the merits and risks of an investment in the Company.

E. **No Reliance on Unauthorized Statements.** The Investor acknowledges and understands, however, that the Company has not authorized any agent or other person to make any statements on its behalf which would in any way contradict any of the information which the Company has provided to the Investor in writing, including the information set forth in this Agreement, the Offering Memorandum and the Shareholder Agreement, and the Investor has not relied upon any such representations regarding the Company, its business or financial condition, or this transaction in making any decision to purchase the Shares. If the Investor becomes aware of conflicting information, the Investor will discuss this with management of the Company.

F. **Solicitation.** The Investor acknowledges that the offer and sale of the Shares has not been accomplished by any form of general solicitation or general advertising, including, but not limited to, any advertisement, article, notice or other communication published in any newspaper, magazine or similar media, or broadcast over television or radio and any seminar or meeting whose attendees have been invited by any general solicitation or general advertising.

G. **Illiquidity; Risk.** The Investor understands that substantial restrictions will exist on transferability of the Shares, that no market for sale of the Shares exists or is expected to develop, and that the Investor may not be able to liquidate its investment in the Company. The Investor understands that any certificates representing the Shares may bear legends restricting the transfer thereof. The Investor understands that investment in the Company entails a very high degree of risk and understands fully the risks associated with the operation of the Company and the Investor's investment in the Company. The Investor represents and warrants that it has adequate means for providing for its current needs and personal contingencies and has no need for liquidity with respect to its investment in the Company.

H. **Economic Loss and Sophistication.** The Investor acknowledges that an investment in the Company pursuant to this Agreement and the Shareholder Agreement involves a high degree of risk and should only be undertaken by persons who can afford to lose the entire amount invested. The Investor is able to bear the economic risk of losing its entire investment in the Company. The Investor's overall commitment to investments that are not readily marketable is not disproportionate to its net worth. The Investor's investment in the Company will not cause such overall commitment to become excessive. The Investor has such knowledge and experience in financial and business matters that he or she is capable of evaluating the risks and merits of this investment.

I. **No Registration of Shares of the Company.** The Investor acknowledges and agrees that, based in part upon its representations and warranties contained herein and in reliance upon applicable exemptions, no Shares in the Company acquired by the Investor have been or will be registered under the Securities Act or the securities laws of any other domestic or foreign jurisdiction. Accordingly, no such Shares may be offered for sale, sold, pledged, hypothecated, or otherwise transferred in whole or in part except in accordance with the terms of the

Shareholder Agreement and in compliance with all applicable laws, including securities laws. The Investor acknowledges that it has been advised that the Company has no obligation and does not intend to cause any Shares in the Company to be registered under the Securities Act or any other securities laws or to comply with any exemption under the Securities Act or any other securities law which would permit the Investor to sell the Shares. The Investor understands and agrees that it must bear the economic risk of its investment for an indefinite period of time.

J. **Principal Place of Business; Organization.** The address for the Investor set forth on the first page of this Agreement is the subscriber's correct principal place of business (or residence if a natural person), and the Investor has no present intention of moving its principal place of business (or residence if a natural person) to any other domestic or foreign jurisdiction. The state and country of the Investor's principal place of business set forth on the Investor's signature page to this Agreement and the state and country of organization are the Investor's correct state and country of the Investor's principal place of business and organization, as the case may be (if the Investor is not a natural person).

K. **Source of Funds.** No part of the funds to be used to purchase and hold the Shares or to pay any amounts under any Subscription Document constitutes an asset of any employee benefit plan in respect of which the Company, or any person considered an employee, agent or affiliate of the Company within the meaning of Section 407(d)(7) of the Employee Retirement Income Security Act of 1974, as amended ("ERISA"), is a party in interest or a disqualified person. As used herein, the terms "employee benefit plan" and "party in interest" shall have the meanings assigned to such terms in Section 3 of ERISA, and the term "disqualified person" shall have the meaning assigned to such term in Section 4975 of the Code.

L. **Benefit Plan Investor Status.** Except as otherwise specified on the Investor's signature page to this Agreement, the Investor is not a "benefit plan investor" (as such term is defined in 29 C.F.R. § 2510.3-101(f)(2)). If the Investor is a benefit plan investor, the plan participants are not permitted to decide whether or how much to invest in particular investment alternatives, and if the Investor is a collective investment vehicle, the plans participating therein do not direct the specific investments made by the Investor.

M. **Investment Company Act.** The Investor understands that the Company has not been registered as an investment company under the Investment Company Act, in reliance upon an exemption from registration thereunder, and the Investor agrees that its Shares may not be sold, offered for sale, transferred, pledged, hypothecated, or otherwise disposed of in any manner that would require the Company to register as an investment company under the Investment Company Act. The Investor has been advised that the Company has no obligation and does not intend to register any interests in the Company.

If the Investor is a corporation, partnership, trust, IRA, Keogh or other employee benefit plan, or other person, then, to the best of its knowledge, based on reasonable investigation, the value of all securities owned by the Investor of all issuers which would be investment companies (as defined under the Investment Company Act) but for the fact that the outstanding securities (other than short-term paper) of such issuer are beneficially owned by not more than 100 persons and such issuer has not made and does not propose to make a public offering of its securities, does not exceed ten percent (10%) of the value of the Investor's total assets.

N. **No Investment or Tax Advice.** The Investor acknowledges that neither the Company nor any agent or affiliate thereof has rendered or will tender any investment advice, securities valuation advice, or tax advice relating to this investment to the Investor, and that the Investor is neither subscribing for nor acquiring any interest in the Company in reliance upon, or with the expectation of, any such advice. The Investor acknowledges that no person was utilized as its purchaser representative in connection with evaluating the merits and risks of the Shares.

O. **Publicly Traded Companies.** Either the Investor is not a company, S corporation, or grantor trust for US federal income tax purposes, or, if the Investor is a company, S corporation, or grantor trust, the Investor was not formed with, and will not be used for, a principal purpose of permitting the Company to satisfy the 100 partner limitation contained in Section 1.7704-1(h)(1)(ii) of the Treasury Regulations promulgated under the Code.

P. **No Violation of Anti-Money Laundering Laws.** No part of the funds used by the Investor to purchase the Shares was directly or indirectly derived from, or related to, any activity that may contravene federal, state or international laws and regulations, including anti-money laundering laws and regulations. The purchase of Shares by the Investor shall not cause the Company or its affiliates to be in violation of any applicable anti-money laundering laws and regulations including the USA Patriot Act of 2001 and regulations of the US Department of the Treasury's Office of Foreign Assets Control ("OFAC").

Q. **OFAC Certification.** The Investor and its affiliates are not acting, directly or indirectly, for or on behalf of any person, group, entity, or nation named by any Executive Order of the US as a terrorist, Specially Designated National and Blocked Person ("SDN") or other banned or blocked person, entity, nation, or transaction, pursuant to any law, order, rule or regulation that is enforced or administered by OFAC. Investor and its affiliates also are not engaged in this transaction, directly or indirectly on behalf of, or instigating or facilitating this transaction, directly or indirectly on behalf of any SDN.

R. **No Reliance on Forward Looking Statements.** Investor acknowledges that the Subscription Documents, including exhibits, contain "forward-looking statements" concerning the plans, intentions, strategies, expectations, predictions and financial forecasts of the Company. Investor understands that such forward-looking statements merely represent the Company's opinion and that the Company's actual results could differ materially from the forward-looking statements. Investor is not relying upon such forward-looking statements when investing in the Company.

S. **Good Standing.** If the Investor is a corporation, limited liability company, partnership, trust, IRA, Keogh or other employee benefit plan, or other entity, the Investor is duly organized, validly existing and in good standing under the laws of the jurisdiction in which it is organized.

T. Formation of Investor. If an entity, the Investor was not formed for the purpose of investing in the Company unless all of the owners of Investor are themselves accredited investors.

U. Effect and Time of Representations. The Investor's representations and agreements set forth in this Agreement and the representations and information furnished in this Agreement are true, correct, and complete and have been complied with, as of the date of the Investor's execution of this Agreement and shall survive its admission as a shareholder of the Company. If in any respect such representations, agreements, and furnished information shall not be true, correct, and complete or shall not have been complied with, as of any date on or before Investor's admission as a shareholder of the Company, the Investor shall promptly give written notice of such fact to the Company and shall specify which representations, agreements, and furnished information are not true, correct, and complete or have not been complied with and the reasons therefor. The Investor acknowledges that the Company, and each respective Shareholder thereof, has relied and will rely upon the representations and agreements of, and information furnished by, the Investor set forth in the Subscription Documents and that all such representations, agreements, and furnished information shall survive the Closing Date.

V. Investor Awareness. The Investor acknowledges, represents, agrees and is aware that:

a.   the Company has a limited financial or operating history;

b.   the Shares have not been registered under the Securities Act or any state or foreign securities laws;

c.   the Company has no obligations to register the Shares;

d.   the Shares are being acquired are, and will continue to be, restricted securities within the meaning of Rule 144 promulgated under the Securities Act and applicable state statutes;

e.   an appropriate restrictive legend or legends will be placed on any certificates evidencing Shares and any certificates issued in replacement or exchange therefor;

f.   the Shares cannot be sold unless they are registered under the Securities Act and any applicable state securities laws or unless an exemption from such registration requirements is available;

g.   the Investor must bear the economic risk of the investment in the Shares for an indefinite period of time because they have not been registered under the Securities Act or any state securities laws;

h.   only the Company may register the Shares under the Securities Act and state securities statutes and the Company has not made any representations to the Investor regarding the registration of the Shares or compliance any exemption under the Securities Act;

i.   the Investor will not sell or attempt to sell the Shares without registration under the Securities Act and any applicable state securities laws, unless exemptions from such registration requirements are available and the Investor has satisfied the Company that an exemption is available for such sale;

j.   except in accordance with the Securities Act, the Company will maintain instructions to bar the transfer of any of the certificates representing the Shares;

k.   no federal or state agency has passed upon the Shares or made any finding or determination as to the fairness of this investment;

l.   the Shareholder Agreement contains substantial restrictions on transferability of the Shares.

V.   COUNSEL TO THE COMPANY

The Investor understands that Legal Law and Esquire LLP acts as counsel to the Company. The Investor also understands that, in connection with this offering of Shares and subsequent advice to the Company, Legal Law and Esquire LLP will not be representing investors in the Company, including the Investor, and no independent counsel has been retained to represent investors in the Company.

The Investor acknowledges that Legal Law and Esquire LLP has not and will not provide any advice to any Investor regarding the taxation of its investment in the Company and that the investor is relying upon its own advisors with respect to these matters.

VI. INDEMNIFICATION

The Investor agrees to indemnify and hold harmless the Company, its officers and directors and each other person, if any, who controls or is controlled by any thereof, within the meaning of Section 15 of the Securities Act, against any and all loss, liability, claim, damage and expense whatsoever (including, but not limited to, any and all expenses whatsoever reasonably incurred in investigating, preparing or defending against any litigation commenced or threatened or any claim whatsoever) arising out of or based upon (1) any false representation or warranty or breach or failure by the Investor to comply with any covenant or agreement made by the Investor, in the Subscription Documents or in any other document furnished by the Investor to any of the foregoing in connection with this transaction or (2) any action for securities law violations instituted by the Investor which is finally resolved by judgment against the Investor.

VII.   POWER OF ATTORNEY

The Investor, as principal, hereby appoints the Chief Executive Officer of the Company as its true and lawful representative and attorney-in-fact, in its name, place and stead to make, execute, sign, acknowledge, swear to and file:

a. any stock certificate, business certificate, fictitious name certificate, amendment thereto, or other instrument or document of any kind necessary or desirable to accomplish the business, purpose and objectives of the Company, or required by any applicable federal, state, or local or foreign law;

b. the Shareholder Agreement and any amendment duly approved as provided therein; and

c. any instruments, certificates and other documents that may be deemed necessary or desirable to affect the winding-up and termination of the Company (including, but not limited to, a Certificate of Dissolution).

This power of attorney is coupled with an interest, is irrevocable, and shall survive and shall not be affected by, the subsequent death, disability, incompetency, termination, bankruptcy, insolvency or dissolution of the Investor; *provided, however,* that this power of attorney will terminate upon the substitution of another shareholder for all of the Investor's investment in the Company, upon the withdrawal of the Investor from the Company or upon the redemption of all of the Shares owned by the Investor.

VIII.   TRUSTEE, AGENT, REPRESENTATIVE OR NOMINEE

If the Investor is acting as trustee, agent, representative or nominee, the Investor understands and acknowledges that the representations, warranties and agreements made herein are made by the Investor with respect to the Investor. The Investor further represents and warrants that it has all requisite power and authority to execute and perform the obligations under this Subscription. The Investor also agrees to indemnify the Company, the Board of Directors and the officers and agents for any and all costs, fees and expenses (including legal fees and disbursements) in connection with any damages resulting from the Investor's misrepresentation or misstatement contained herein, or the assertion of the Investor's lack of proper authorization to enter into this Subscription Agreement or perform the obligations hereof.

IX. GENERAL MATTERS.

A. **Amendments**. This Agreement may be modified or amended only with the prior written consent of the Company.

B. **Notices**. Any notice, request, demand, or other communication required by or permitted to be given in connection with this Agreement shall be in writing, except as expressly otherwise permitted herein, and shall be delivered in person, sent by first class mail (postage prepaid and certified or registered, with return receipt requested), sent by facsimile or similar means of communication, or delivered by a courier service (charges prepaid), addressed to the parties at the respective addresses (or such other address as such party may give to the others in writing) set forth on Page SA-1 of this Subscription Agreement. Any such notice, request, demand, or other communication shall be deemed to be given (i) when received, if personally delivered; (ii) if mailed, on the third day after it is deposited in the United States mail, properly addressed, with proper postage affixed; (iii) if sent by facsimile or similar device, when electronically confirmed; and (iv) if sent by courier, 24 hours after delivery to such courier service.

C. **Governing Law; Assignment; Binding Effect; and Severability.** This Agreement shall be enforced, governed, and construed in all respects in accordance with the laws of the State of Colorado applicable to contracts executed and performable solely in such state. The Investor irrevocably submits to the personal jurisdiction of the federal and state courts of Colorado. The Investor may not assign any of its rights or obligations under this Agreement without the prior written consent of the Company. This Agreement and the rights and obligations set forth herein shall be binding upon, and shall inure to the benefit of, the Investor, the Company, and their respective legal representatives, successors, and permitted assigns. If the Investor is more than one person, the obligation of the Investor shall be joint and several and the agreements, representations, warranties and acknowledgments herein contained shall be deemed to be made by and be binding upon each such person and his heirs, executors, administrators and successors. If any provision of this Agreement, or the application of such provision to any circumstance, shall be invalid under the applicable law of any jurisdiction, the remainder of this Agreement or the application of such provision to other persons or circumstances or in other jurisdictions shall not be affected thereby.

D. **Entire Agreement.** This Agreement and any other agreements between the Company and the Investor (it being acknowledged and agreed that the Company may enter into other agreements with the Investor in order to meet certain requirements of the Investor) constitute the entire agreement of the parties hereto in respect of the subject matter hereof, and supersede all prior agreements or understandings, among the parties hereto in respect of the subject matter hereof.

E. **Counterparts**. This Agreement may be executed in multiple counterparts, each of which when so executed shall be deemed to be an original and all of which taken together shall constitute one and the same agreement.

F. **Further Assurances; Additional Documentation**. The Investor agrees to execute any additional documents and agreements to complete its subscription, as defined in the Shareholder Agreement.

G. **Conflicts**. In the event of any conflict between the Shareholder Agreement and this Agreement, the Shareholder Agreement shall control.

X. ADDITIONAL INFORMATION AND SUBSEQUENT CHANGES IN THE FOREGOING REPRESENTATIONS

The Company may request from the Investor such additional information as it may deem necessary to evaluate the eligibility of the Investor to acquire an Interest, and may request from time to time such information as it may deem necessary to determine the eligibility of the Investor to hold an Interest or to enable the Company to determine the Company's compliance with applicable regulatory requirements, and the Investor shall provide such information as may reasonably be requested.

Each person acquiring an Interest must satisfy the foregoing both at the time of subscription and at all times thereafter until such person ceases to be a Shareholder of the Company. Accordingly, the Investor agrees to notify the Company promptly if there is any change with respect to any of the foregoing information or representations and to provide the Company with such further information as the Company may reasonably require.

[BALANCE OF PAGE INTENTIONALLY LEFT BLANK.
SIGNATURE PAGE FOLLOWS]

ABC INC.

SUBSCRIPTION AGREEMENT SIGNATURE PAGE

IN WITNESS WHEREOF, the Investor has executed this Subscription Agreement as of the date set forth below, and with respect to the information disclosed in Item III of this Subscription Agreement, has executed this Subscription Agreement under penalties of perjury.

Date: _____, 20___

For Individual Investors:

For Investors other than Individuals:

_____
(Please Type Name of Investor)

_____
Signature

_____
(Please Type Name)

By: _____
Signature

_____
(Please Type Name of Signatory)

Title: _____

SUBSCRIPTION ACCEPTED:

ABC INC.

Date: _____

By: _____
Name: Fred Jones
Title: CEO

ABC INC.

EXHIBIT A – SHAREHOLDER AGREEMENT

(Attached)

ABC INC.

EXHIBIT B –OFFERING MEMORANDUM

(Attached)

APPENDIX D

REGULATION D RULE 506(D) BAD BOY CERTIFICATE

The following is an example of a typical "Bad Boy" certificate for Rule 506 offerings. Each officer, director, beneficial owner of 20 percent or more and other party described in the certificate should execute a certificate to confirm that they are unaware of any facts that would disqualify the issuer from relying on an exemption pursuant to Rule 506. In the case of an offering pursuant to Regulation D Rule 505, the compliance certificate should list all of the disqualifying events under Regulation A Rule 262 described in Chapter 5. Check with your legal counsel for details.

REGULATION D RULE 506 COMPLIANCE CERTIFICATE

XYZ, Inc. ("Issuer") plans to sell its securities in an offering pursuant to the exemption provided by Rule 506 of Regulation D of the Securities Act of 1933.

In furtherance of this offering, the executive officers, directors, and beneficial owners of more than 20 percent of the Issuer's outstanding voting securities have agreed to certify to their belief that the Issuer is not disqualified from relying on the Rule 506 exemption.

I. [NAME OF PERSON CERTIFYING], am the [TITLE OF PERSON CERTIFYING] of the Issuer, and I hereby certify that to my knowledge, neither the Issuer, any predecessor of the Issuer or affiliated Issuer; nor any director, executive officer, other officer participating in the offering, [general partner or managing member of the issuer]; any beneficial owner of 20 percent or more of the issuer's outstanding voting equity securities; [any promoter connected with the issuer in any capacity at the time of such sale; any investment manager of an issuer that is a pooled investment fund; any person that has been or will be paid (directly or indirectly) remuneration for solicitation of purchasers in connection with such sale of securities; any general partner or managing member of any such investment manager or solicitor; or any director, executive officer or other officer participating in the offering of any such investment manager or solicitor or general partner or managing member of such investment manager or solicitor][REVISE LIST AS APPROPRIATE]:

1. Has been convicted, within ten years before such sale (or five years, in the case of the Issuer, its predecessors and affiliated issuers), of any felony or misdemeanor:

   a. In connection with the purchase or sale of any security;
   b. Involving the making of any false filing with the Securities and Exchange Commission (the "Commission"); or
   c. Arising out of the conduct of the business of an underwriter, broker, dealer, municipal securities dealer, investment adviser or paid solicitor of purchasers of securities;

2. Is subject to any order, judgment or decree of any court of competent jurisdiction, entered within five years before such sale, that, at the time of such sale, restrains or enjoins such person from engaging or continuing to engage in any conduct or practice:

   a. In connection with the purchase or sale of any security;
   b. Involving the making of any false filing with the Commission; or
   c. Arising out of the conduct of the business of an underwriter, broker, dealer, municipal securities dealer, investment adviser or paid solicitor of purchasers of securities;

3. Is subject to a final order of a state securities commission (or an agency or officer of a state authority performing like functions); a state authority that supervises or examines banks, savings associations, or credit unions; a state insurance commission (or an agency or officer of a state performing like functions); an appropriate federal banking agency; the US Commodity Futures Trading Commission; or the National Credit Union Administration that:

   a. At the time of such sale, bars the person from:

      i. Association with an entity regulated by such commission, authority, agency, or officer;

ii. Engaging in the business of securities, insurance or banking; or

iii. Engaging in savings association or credit union activities; or

b. Constitutes a final order based on a violation of any law or regulation that prohibits fraudulent, manipulative, or deceptive conduct entered within ten years before such sale;

4. Is subject to an order of the Commission entered pursuant to section 15(b) or 15B(c) of the Securities Exchange Act of 1934 (15 U.S.C. 78o(b) or 78o-4(c)) or section 203(e) or (f) of the Investment Advisers Act of 1940 (15 U.S.C. 80b-3(e) or (f)) that, at the time of such sale:

a. Suspends or revokes such person's registration as a broker, dealer, municipal securities dealer or investment adviser;

b. Places limitations on the activities, functions or operations of such person; or

c. Bars such person from being associated with any entity or from participating in the offering of any penny stock;

5. Is subject to any order of the Commission entered within five years before such sale that, at the time of such sale, orders the person to cease and desist from committing or causing a violation or future violation of:

a. Any scienter-based anti-fraud provision of the federal securities laws, including without limitation section 17(a)(1) of the Securities Act of 1933 (15 U.S.C. 77q(a)(1)), section 10(b) of the Securities Exchange Act of 1934 (15 U.S.C. 78j(b)) and 17 CFR 240.10b-5, section 15(c)(1) of the Securities Exchange Act of 1934 (15 U.S.C. 78o(c)(1)) and section 206(1) of the Investment Advisers Act of 1940 (15 U.S.C. 80b-6(1)), or any other rule or regulation thereunder; or

b. Section 5 of the Securities Act of 1933 (15 U.S.C. 77e).

6. Is suspended or expelled from membership in, or suspended or barred from association with a member of, a registered national securities exchange or a registered national or affiliated securities association for any act or omission to act constituting conduct inconsistent with just and equitable principles of trade;

7. Has filed (as a registrant or issuer), or was named as an underwriter in, any registration statement or Regulation A offering statement filed with the Commission that, within five years before such sale, was the subject of a refusal order, stop order, or order suspending the Regulation A exemption, or is, at the time of such sale, the subject of an investigation or proceeding to determine whether a stop order or suspension order should be issued;

8. Is subject to a United States Postal Service false representation order entered within five years before such sale, or is, at the time of such sale, subject to a temporary restraining order or preliminary injunction with respect to conduct alleged by the United States Postal Service to constitute a scheme or device for obtaining money or property through the mail by means of false representations; or

9. Is subject to any order, judgment or decree of any court of competent jurisdiction temporarily, preliminarily or permanently enjoining such person for failure to comply with §230.503.

The statements contained in this Certificate are based upon my familiarity with the business, operations, and other affairs of the Issuer, which familiarity is sufficient to enable the undersigned to express an informed judgment as to the matters set forth herein.

The undersigned has executed this Officer's Certificate effective the ___ day of _____ 20__ .

_____

[NAME, TITLE OF CERTIFYING PERSON]

APPENDIX E

BOARD RESOLUTIONS AUTHORIZING A PRIVATE PLACEMENT OFFERING

UNANIMOUS WRITTEN CONSENT OF THE BOARD OF DIRECTORS OF XYZ, INC. IN LIEU OF SPECIAL MEETING

The undersigned, being all of the members of the board of directors (the "Board") of XYZ, Inc., a Colorado corporation (the "Company"), do hereby consent, pursuant to Section 7-108-202 of the Colorado Business Corporation Act (the "Act"), to the adoption of the following resolutions and agree that said resolutions shall have the same effect as if duly adopted at a special meeting held for that purpose:

RECITALS

A. The Company considers it necessary, appropriate and desirable to offer for sale, and to sell, up to 50,000 shares of its common stock, no par value per share (the "Common Stock"), in an offering intended to be exempt from registration under the Securities Act of 1933, as amended (the "Securities Act") and Regulation D of the Securities Act (the "Offering"); and

B. In accordance with the Offering, the Company intends to offer for sale and sell shares of Common Stock to certain investors as contemplated by the Subscription Documents referred to below and to take all steps necessary to ensure that such offers and sales are in compliance with applicable state and federal law.

RESOLUTIONS

NOW THEREFORE, be it

OFFERING MEMORANDUM

RESOLVED, that in connection with the Offering, the Chairman of the Board, the President, and the Treasurer of the Company (each, a "Proper

Officer") of the Company be, and each of them acting individually hereby is, authorized and directed in the name and on behalf of the Company to prepare and deliver, or cause to be prepared and delivered, an Offering Memorandum relating to the Offering, substantially in the form attached hereto as **Exhibit A** ("Offering Memorandum"), including any revisions thereof and amendments and supplements to the Offering Memorandum containing such necessary information, exhibits and other documents;

RESOLVED, that the form, terms and provisions of a Subscription Agreement to be entered into by and between the Company and certain investors (the "Investors"), providing for the purchase by the Investors of the shares of Common Stock in a transaction not involving a public offering on the terms and conditions set forth therein (the "Subscription Agreement"), substantially in the form as included in the Offering Memorandum, be, and the same hereby are, approved, and the Proper Officers are authorized and directed to execute and deliver one or more Subscription Agreements with such modifications, amendments or changes therein as the Proper Officer executing the same may approve;

THE OFFERING

RESOLVED, that the sale and issuance of shares of Common Stock in the Offering pursuant to the terms and conditions set forth in the Offering Memorandum and the Subscription Agreements and related documents are hereby approved, and that up to 50,000 shares of Common Stock, be, and they hereby are, reserved for such purposes;

RESOLVED, that the Company is authorized to issue from time to time in accordance with the Subscription Agreements such number of shares of Common Stock as may be otherwise issuable from time to time in accordance with the terms of the Subscription Agreement, and the consideration for the shares of Common Stock as expressed in the Subscription Agreements is deemed adequate;

RESOLVED, that the Proper Officers are authorized and directed to issue or cause to be issued appropriate stock certificates representing such shares of Common Stock, and that, when issued in accordance with the terms of the Subscription Agreements and upon payment for such shares as provided in the Subscription Agreements, such shares shall be validly issued, fully paid and non-assessable;

BLUE SKY FILINGS

RESOLVED, that the Proper Officers are authorized and empowered to prepare and file Form with the Securities and Exchange Commission and any states where such filing is necessary with respect to the exemption from registration of the shares of Common Stock issuable in the Offering and to pay all such fees and expenses as may be required under such laws, and to take any and all further action which they may deem necessary or advisable in order to maintain such exemption in effect for as long as they deem to be in the best interests of the Company;

RATIFICATION OF PRIOR ACTIONS

RESOLVED, that any actions taken by any of the Proper Officers or by any employees or agents of the Company on or prior to the date on which the Board of Directors adopted the foregoing resolutions in connection with the Offering and the transactions contemplated by these resolutions are ratified, confirmed and approved;

GENERAL

RESOLVED, that the Proper Officers of the Company are authorized and empowered, in the name and on behalf of the Company, to take all such further action and do such things, and to execute and deliver all such agreements, certificates, consents, instruments and documents and to prepare or cause to be prepared, execute and file or cause to be filed with any federal, state, local, foreign or other regulatory agencies any forms, reports, filings, applications or other documents, and to make all expenditures and incur all expenses which such Proper Officers, in their discretion deem necessary, desirable or appropriate to carry out fully the foregoing resolutions and the purposes and intents thereof; and

RESOLVED, that this written consent may be executed by fax, e-mail, or otherwise in one or more counterparts, each of which shall be deemed an original, but which shall together constitute one and the same document.

[REMAINDER OF PAGE INTENTIONALLY LEFT BLANK]

This Consent may be signed in one or more counterparts, each of which shall be deemed an original, and all of which shall constitute one instrument. This Consent shall be filed with the minutes of the proceedings of the Board of Directors of the Company.

The undersigned have executed this Consent to be effective as of _____ ___, 20__ .

                                      _____,
                                        Director

                                        _____,
                                        Director

APPENDIX F

PPM TABLE OF CONTENTS

Every Private Placement Memorandum is different and the information that should be included will vary significantly depending on the exemption relied upon, whether the offering includes unaccredited investors and the nature of the issuer and the offering. This is an example of a typical table of contents for a Private Placement Memorandum for a company like XYZ.

TABLE OF CONTENTS

I. Summary of the Offering
II. Investor Qualifications
III. Risk Factors
IV. Description of the Company
V. Business Plan
VI. Use of Proceeds
VII. Investment Objectives
VIII. Terms of the Offering
IX. Management
X. The Investment Placement Agent
XI. Conflicts of Interest
XII. Tax Considerations
XIII. Transfer Restrictions
XIV. Summary of the Company's Governance Documents
XV. Legal Proceedings
XVI. Company Financial Statements
XVII. Additional Information and Other Matters

Exhibits

Exhibit A   Articles, Bylaws and Shareholder Agreement
Exhibit B   Form of Subscription Agreement

ABOUT THE AUTHOR

Jacqueline M. Benson is an Of Counsel attorney at Moye White LLP in Denver, Colorado, and vice chair of the firm's Securities and Capital Markets Group. She has experience representing public and private companies in state and federal securities compliance, business planning and formation, financing, mergers and acquisitions, asset and stock sales, corporate governance and restructuring transactions. She also has experience with securities litigation and commercial disputes and represents clients before the Securities and Exchange Commission and Public Company Accounting Oversight Board. In her spare time, she plays hockey and volunteers with golden retriever rescue.

ASPATORE